津浪

This House

This House

A Poem in Seven Books

by

Jim Bodeen

With Photographs by Rob Prout

Tsunami Inc.
Walla Walla, Washington

Acknowledgments

PUTTING MY BELT BUCKLE BACK ON MY BELT, I SAY TO THE CRAFTSMAN, 'IF I HAD THESE JEWELS INSIDE ME NOW I MIGHT NOT NEED THE ADORNMENT ON THE OUTSIDE; THIS IS THE LESSON IN THE JEWELRY, originally appeared in Crab Creek Review

Praise and gratitude to everyone who came into my life during the creation of this poem. Zev, Barry, Marty, Raúl, Tom; Judy, Gayle, Joan, Janeen; Mom, Tim & Shannon, Leah, Krista & Ricardo; Roland Dougherty, the Waterman; for Pastor Harald Sigmar, and Ethel; Jan, the dog lady; Cy & Rosemary; Bonnie, Carolyn; the abrecaminos: Javier, Yoshimi, Alma, Eva Siddhartha, all of you; for the poets and poetry; for jazz, especially John Coltrane, who shows us a way. For Charles Potts and his grand vision of the big wave.

Lee Bassett, Frank Malgesini, Sylvia Trejo, Raúl Torres, Gayle Kaune, Kevin Miller, Harris Levinson and Ed Stover, read the manuscript and gave valuable suggestions. They are not responsible for what I do with the dream. Raúl Torres, worked with me on the Spanish, and Frank Malgesini and Sylvia Trejos of the University of Chihuahua, made improvements with differing practices in usage, mil gracias.

For permission to use "Yes swells in our soul," from the CD, *In This House, On This Morning* by Wynton Marsalis Septet, thank you.

Thanks to Rob Prout, for his attention to the work and the photographs.

ISBN: 0-9644440-6-2

Tsunami Inc.
PO Box 100, Walla Walla, WA 99362-0033
http://www.wwics.com/~tsunami> <tsunami@wwics.com>

for Karen,
and for the dream—
everything else is orthodoxy

Table of Contents

BOOK ONE

This Path, This Garden, This House

Book One

This old garage out back, this grape-covered hut,
sends out trumpets and drums into the dark crisp air of pre-dawn.
The far stars are present, but neither witness nor interfere,
and it is too late and too early for jazz, a perfect time.
The village sleeps. I am up, out back,
a charmed man, and in the mornings before the village
starts to wake and cling, I am called by the horn. The trumpet player
is the only man in his band not raised in a church.
All summer long I waited for this poem to get up and write its way
into me from the garden, a lyric dream connected by color and blossom,
and now, from this solitary light before the ancient gears
of the old press, surrounded by white walls, it beckons
to a man torn and charmed, in between time, liminal.

In this house, my beloved wife, the maker
of the sacred vests, turns between sleeping and waking.
Downstairs, Ella Fitzgerald sings from the songbooks
in the first crisp fall after her crossing.
Here, as in a daydream I stand. What stars foretold...
Sleeping between Karen and the puppy, I'm told
in yet another dream, the death exchange must be complete
for the survival of the poem. I throw a stick into the river.
The word for a sheet of paper in Spanish comes from the trees.
Hojas, leaves. Take a leaf from a tree, and a feather from a bird,
and some juice from a berry. I defend this line against
all comers: each of us is born with a box of matches inside,
but we can't strike them by ourselves. Dip the feather
in the juice, touch the leaf. My friend's voice
arrives in the new mail, My dad called and ordered my book.
Karen hears me weeping in the garden. It's not easier
being a rabbi's son, she says, no easier

than being the son of Wayne Bodeen. Rejoice.
The best bass player in the world, Ray Brown,
plays in my living room. *Take the A Train.* Sacred journey.
La jornada sagrada. Manda. Peregrinaje.
I have been on a long climb with *la Raza.*
Sacred climb, sacred place. The Macchu Picchu of our pierced hearts.
In this house, on this morning, I pay homage at the stone altar.
Gabino Salazar, stops me as we walk. *I am Indian,* he says.
Oaxaqueño, he has never seen the ruins at Mitla.
Tan lejos de mi pueblo. The word for water, *Chicui.*
Thousands of miles. More years than miles.
Tens of thousands of years.
And what language do you speak with your mother?
I tell her about each day, he says. *I speak in her language.*
Her son's daily voice visits her in the *barranca seca.*
He tells her everything each day.
A woman's voice comes up in the strings,
Tell them I am the bird's nest behind the waterfall.

Lacy Dreamwalker, the Black Lab pup, in a Down Stay
at my feet, looks straight at the trumpet coming into her ears.
I am thinking of men. A woman has sent me her paper,
Sunken Dirt In The Bullet Hole. She is working to help veterans
heal from trauma. We have been talking about families.
Marsalis plays the Lord's Prayer. A friend says to a friend,
I want to have the political ability to talk to colleagues.
I want to know how to compromise in my own house.
The friend says, Don't compromise. Politicians we trust
have all resigned. I don't want you to compromise.
I counter with another truth, equally small,
the rage comes from the impotency of not being listened to.
Separation gives us a chance to be ourselves. This is love.
This morning I want to hear the voice in the horn say yes.
I want to find a way to friends without prescription.
I want to find a way to talk of the terror.

Camina conmigo the t-shirt read, and I wanted it
for those words. My desire, and willingness to be led.
I am following the Mexicans into my own story. Wine grapes,
crushed and cooked yesterday for today's jelly,
wait for me in the refrigerator. In the *sweet embrace
of life.* A saxophone, a human voice, and a drum.

Over and over. I have been waking in this house
for 25 years. My daughters have never lived
in another house. Waking up. Three women
are upstairs sleeping. Straining the rich juice
through cheese cloth, staring into the emerging
clarity of its red, and almost black, burgundy:
The Jelly of Memory and Forgetting.
What does it take to wake us from our sleep?

Sitting in front of a silent television
I type my mother's Christmas letter while my wife
listens to her talk in the living room. In last night's dream,
I'm unsettled, dancing around a woman who wants to know
if she has a place to live. Stop, she says, Give me a direct answer.
All of the women want answers. I'm some kind of bureaucrat.
What does this dream have to do with me? All of the women
in this house are waking up. In this house, on this morning,
it is Thanksgiving. Pay attention. It must have something to do
with the miser. If I can't receive I must not be the giver
I think I am. Just the other night I am the thief again,
stealing blackberry vines to cook into a paper to bind
a book. I cut and pull the vines from rocks.
The best provider is the dreamer turned into bureaucrat.
Cutting stems from other herbs, the plants become
the book spine, the backbone of literature.
The steering wheel of the dream ties itself to freedom.

We are pilgrims. The dream is a foothold
on the crumbling rock of truth. Psyche first shows
in the final scene of three One Acts.
I'm at a softball game watching from the sidelines
in a lawn chair, a character in my own dream.
A little girl, a child, somewhere around five,
naked except for panties, walks over to me,
puts her leg over my shoulders
as if she's dancing. I ask her,
Who have you done this with before me?
She says, My father, and runs away.
She runs around the bases laughing.
I follow, confused. I'm not the father in this dream.
As I cross home plate, she has disappeared.
Looking around, I get hit by a foul ball

in the back of my neck. My bell is really rung.
A man who interprets dreams asks me
about my life five years ago. I tell him about the seizure.
It's her, he says, Psyche. The music of birds.

Karen comes downstairs in the morning
for coffee and the paper. The Secret Room,
she says, *I almost forgot to tell you about it.*
In an attic, in Indiana, I think, but not Mary's house.
Not any house I know, but in this room, refuge.
room for me, me to be me, and only love.
In this house, in this attic room, she claims herself.
I almost forgot them, the dream, the Secret Room.
The truth is, there is no orthodoxy in dreams.
The Executive Mother surrounded by telephones is only herself.
Karen takes all calls. Listens to any story.
She takes the grief into her dream.
I sit before the sacred, a witness.
Grief gives her the courage. The spiritual mother
becomes the woman in the living room.

The music of monks, teeth on bone.
His morning, early winter,
the best coffee from the poorest countries,
a quiet house. I bring myself.
It is never the same. It is always the same.
A choir boy's life. Ocean prairie.
The songs in the photo album.
Where does the voice come from?
I create the sound by the intent of my listening.
This is the song of the fallen angel.
The only song is the song of myself.
The secret of the universe is sacrifice.
I give up my children. I give them su propia lucha,
their own struggle, a chance to become.

Praise doesn't shun winter's heartbeat.
Praise doesn't control the dream; praise
welcomes what comes. A soccer ball shot
from the canon shakes me down. Make safe passage.
Lacy Dreamwalker wants in from outside. Upstairs
in her bed, my wife uses my pen to write her dream.

Marsalis puts a mute in his horn to clear away clouds.
A woman named Kani visits me between a tennis match
and a poem. She tells me I'm too mean
with my inside me to get out of the dream.
This is a dream inside a dream. It snows outside.
Rewiring this house seems so simple it turns into mystery.
I want Orpheus and Jesus. I get Little Bo Peep.
The Waterman has to sing me the rhyme,
Leave them alone and they'll come home...
A shepherdess. Wailing for her lost daughters. *They'll come home.*

To take what is given: home, dwelling place, calling.
Mi prieta Linda, ¿Qué voy hacer?
The country singer who sang rock and roll,
a Stone Pony, has discovered songs her father loved.
Threshold people. On this morning, in this house,
to stand, humbled and stunned and silent, before the wild
beauty, the mysteries of the women swirling in this house.
The one name, a different drummer, I carried home from Nam.
Mystical, ecstatic praise of wrong action.
I sleep between my wife and my dog, sending the pup
into the marriage bed to wake the wife,
Kiss her Lacy, lick her all over, get her ready for the day.
Singing from a liminal world, the addiction to perfection
is only the call from the angel.

Better get hit in your soul—how, it detests innocence
at any age. What are my defining moments as a parent?
The Sundance drums filter the question.
Defining moments can only be about me.
I am called by the tambourine. Justice and mercy
are such small lights. A Christmas light on a cut tree
placed in a living room. Listen to the bass.
A car's tires spin in the ice from the street below,
calling me from my dream. 5 am. A woman
is stuck in ice. We're unable to push her out.
The woman, in her sixties, steps
from her car breaking into ankle deep icy water.
Her son, a man my son's age, stays with the car.
The car is chained up, and sunk to its axle in ice.
Driving her to work in the nursing home,
she carries her Christmas gifts,

she tells her story, her grandson's death
this summer, the helicopter that came too late.
My pup sleeps through it all. My daughters
are home from the university. My note tells them
they have the keys to all they need.

The pickpocket, whose training is most rigorous,
longer than the physician's, works without insurance.
I am doubly blessed, called from the other world
in the upstairs room where I am a receiver of dreams,
it is my daughter. She, too, is charmed and called,
and calls from an earlier state of receivership.
She tells me what has happened. Her sister calls.
The calls keep coming and I take them all.
My wife asks who is calling and returns to sleep.
My pup, who sleeps by my bed, wants to go out and pee.
Rising to take her out, I am pulled down by my wife.
She wants to make love. She is wet from her dreams.
She tells me this later. She hasn't felt like this in years.
It felt so good on the way down.
Feeding the pup, I remember, I too have been dreaming.
I, even I, in union with my clenched hand.
I embrace myself, I pour seed in my mouth.

Exact language, mysterious reality.
Don't jump to the solution that you understand
because you can relate it to something you know.
Sleeping between my pup and my wife
I have been called. I have been given vocations
from different worlds. I give all I have
to wife and pup. Brave forest, my heart is my own.
I would rather have my wife's dream than her cunt.
This fact comes from the dream, but it is not the dream.
It is a reflection. It is my statement made in conversation.
I do not deny the cunt. The dream is not prosaic mind.
It is not as prosaic as your cultural mentality.
It is the expression of the inexpressible.

The Wilkamaya and the Urubamba.
Two rivers below Macchu Picchu.
We've crossed these, *mis compañeros y yo.*
We do not forget Pinochet

banishing the word in Neruda's Chile.
We're not talking about the *Rio Bravo*.
We've crossed the *Rio Bravo*, too.
All river crossings change the world.
Every bush is on fire. My compañeros
live their lives in metaphor, have the poems
of Rosario Castellanos for maps, *en el presente,*
para no traicionar lo nuestro,
esta luz con que se mira entero.
This day and this light with which
one sees all things. You must be in love
to change your life. Urubamba.
Otra manera de ser. Wilkamayu.

My friend and I sit on tall stools passing Merton
back and forth playing Desert Fathers.
For three years Abbot Agatho places stones
in his mouth to keep silence. Winter solstice,
and the slow descent down the Kabbalist tree.
The priest tells a sinner to leave the community.
Abbot Bessarion gets up and leaves with him,
I too am a sinner. The soul doesn't want
to get messed up in the world. My wife
reads the paper to me. I wince,
give my puppy a bone. My friend wins
with this: Two elders don't know
how to quarrel. They place a brick
between them, practice saying,
It is mine, trying to get angry. But one says,
Then it is yours, and they remain friends.
Might I shed the false self completely, die,
chart my own way to God,
and lighten up just a smidgen, enough
for any mother's son in a Christmas picture.

Lacy Dreamwalker, who graduated from Obedience School
with a diploma earlier today, is from the litter of
R. J.'s Redside Christine and Stephen's Sweet Sage.
Be neither persuaded nor dismayed. She maintains her nature.
Her competencies defy obedience. The purpose
of this Black Lab, this dreamtime pedigree,
is to reveal the nature of man. The line before Chrisie

gave birth to eleven, starts with Buckler's Golden Honey
and Candlewoods Super Tanker. The past includes
hunters who named one pup Mallard Lake Aim And Fire.
And in the middle of this tracked history,
one breeder strove to unite the heiretic and the demotic,
bringing together the Grand Duke of Jackson
with Tasha of T-Town. Chances the Duke was a fraud
are high. The one pure golden union,
if we are to believe names, came earlier
with Mac's Crackerjack and Brad's Golden Lady.
Lacy is destined for the trail, back country. She maps
the wilderness that comes up in me. Great, great
grand sire of San Joachin Honcho and Candlewoods
Delta Dash, Code Red and the original Mallard Lake Kacie,
Lacy Dreamwalker has been bred and tracked
to my doorstep. She is a theory of composition.
This is her pedigree, and her legacy
Begins and ends in ragged lines spilling from dreams.

•

ON THIS TRIP TO MACCHU PICCHU

para mis 52 compañeros

Because I've told him about you
A man says I sound like a man returning
from another world, telling a hallucinogenic story.
I tell it through your poems.
The agent is your inspired breathing.
I tell it through the month spent on the trail.
The lugar sagrado, jornada sagrada. Jóvenes sagrados.
Marisela Farías begins, The flowers of June
developed so natural, like an innocent child.
We've left so many behind, the ones, José Lozano says, who
piensan siempre mal de otros. Those whose *palabras*
son balas—nada más que burlas y gestos.
In the great tradition of romance, Israel Ceja,
beginning his journey, invokes the woman,
la rosa más bella. It's the day of the voyage.

Alma smells grandma's tortillas...
deja la puerta abierta.
The cats will probably go in. And just this fast,
Nada, Muerte es nada. Death you are the shortest trip.
I've got the eye teeth of the lion
bleeding in my hands. I have taken off
the lion's skin, I have the cuernos of the bull.
This is Alma. David Gutiérrez is jumpy,
My indigenous soul panics.
Our spirit gets hit. This is my bullet, too.
Alrededor del jardín, Marta Huerta witnesses,
pecados y culpa. Como cadenas. Adriana urges,
Nunca llega tarde, but sometimes
we invite it to come join us a little sooner.
My actions kill me. I am my own death.
A mother hears her own child cry.
My body *está entumido*
and my eyes are *marchitos.*
Norma Mendoza writes a freedom poem.
She is a work of courage.

My climb to be a man.
Pedro Hernández carves a title in stone.
He says goodby to friends, loses the mother
who gave him birth, and remembers
crossing a river in Michoacán to get papayas.
Crossing three borders, Juan Arévalo, our *el Salvadoreño,*
says it wasn't easy getting here.
Efren Chacón says:
I do not see any *miedo en mis ojos.*
I do not see *vergueñza entre mis compañeros.*
I do not see people saying, I can't.
These are the river crossers.
Alfredo Barriga: *Perdóname, México, por haberte dejado.*
Abandonarte no fue mi intención.
Rachel Casteneda: The deep cut it made was in my heart.
Juan Villegas: *para ver si puedo caminar.*
Erika Fuentes: *Fuerte como la tierra, alma como Indio.*
Rodolfo Camarillo: *Para estudiar.* I take my books and all my works.
Luis Vásquez. Hurt is the price for feeling. Pain is not accident.

Guadalupe Hernández grieves for everyone in Aranza, Michoacán.

Lágrimas y silencio.
La nieve te está cubriendo blanco tu negro pelo.

She makes her father in words. She saves him.

And Eva. Breaking silence.

Silencio, oh maldito Silencio. Compañero.

Volverá a empezar, y a vivir, volverá a soñar.

Her twelve poems holding all of the answers she'll ever need.

Lucha total.

Javier Vargas becomes a man. *Adiós niñez.*
He walks without fear. He walks with fear.
Surrounded by those who live in death
and hold on to luck.

Perfectly bilingual.
Perfectly bicultural.
A national treasure.
Endangered species.

Yoshimi Varela calls it a blue place,
ya no existe anymore.

People are going to be afraid of Yoshimi.

The ruins are beautiful.

Luis writes for his father.
The grandfather needs his father
para sembrar el maíz.
The father works so his son can learn to read.
I was *triste* when I left he says,
now I see a soccer ball wherever I am.
The soccer ball is the earth.
Antonio Oseguera begins late.
He has been in the apples.

Quisiera caminar lejos y comprar flores.
I hear your voice when I dream.

Oscar López carries the black life on his back.

He works in ink.

A list of narrative voices longer than your life.

Alma asks me how come I'm not returning the poems.

I'm still reading them, still taking them into my dreams.
I'm still confused about their gift, still waking at night.

When Israel García leaves a year ago, I begin a letter to the School Board.
I did not send it. Is this an act of self-betrayal?

Gabino Salazar is Mixteco.
He gives us the word for water.
His pueblo is *tan lejos de Oaxaca.*
He has never seen the ruins of Monte Albán.
In the Yakima Valley he comes to see them as *metáforas.*
Triste y solo estuve en
aquella montaña rodeado
de dulces recuerdos.
Trying to experience his solitude
for the length of a phone call
I think of his mother, one of a handful
in this Valley whose every image
is in a language she cannot share.
Gabino interrupts the order of the class reading.
He says I think I can read it all.
He will take this day home to his mother.
This is his *tarea.*
He teaches us about the *magos*
who interpret the sky
the year Cortés arrives.
He writes, ten years ago
I began to understand
what's going on in my life.
Days after my father died,
I was six years old, we left Rio Verde,

looking for a job. Now I am beginning
to understand love.

Telling Gabino's story
to another class, Hortencia Méndez
says Gabino knows the word for water, *ti qui,*
but spells it *tan horrible.*

Israel García's poems win the Raymond Carver writing award.
Carver, *un poeta que se graduó de esta escuela,*
escribió cuentos y poemas que no podemos usar en nuestra escuela.
Looking at a book of Carver's life in Yakima,
Israel says, For the first time I feel I belong.
Israel is not here with papers, legally. He returns to Mexico to study.

Miriam López, the *abrecamino* who first
unmasked the sexual torrents in Neruda,
and brought the flower direct into the classroom
with her expressive, Ah, now says,
No tienes ninguna alternativa. Tienes que luchar.
And this is her Macchu Picchu.
Not to betray her *propia lucha.*

Juan Tejeda's poem is a rap vision he calls Real Poem.

Alba Méndez knows she has things in her pack she doesn't need.
It makes her angry to carry this stuff. Emptying out,
she sees a woman being born.
Gavicel Antúñez sees her spirit die when she doesn't laugh.
Miriam Diáz sees *el silencio del ácido que tiene*
que provocar una obscuridad, titles her journey, In Me.
Efren Chacón *quien tiene tres años de escuela,*
dos aquí y uno en Mexico, 18, stands before the class and reads,
I see a lot of people looking at me, whispering to each other,
saying, look at the boy *con el coraje*
en su cara, tratando de acabar
con las crueles dudas de la vida.
We are not naive.
Ramon Sánchez writes,
When I get to the top
I know everything is not finished.
Pablo López is from Silver River.

He has learned to listen to his mother.
His is a true story.
Norma Mendoza knows her child hears her cry.
Las páginas de mi vida come from Cindy García.
Jesús Soto begins two weeks late and catches up.
María Muñiz walks through chemotherapy.
Her tears are for her parents.
This is *la luz de mi vida:*
Macchu Picchu came,
revealing the path I forgot, the divine origin,
I see the love now, I do not see my illness.
Lines, rhythms, *la mezcla de idiomas,*
todos hacen un mundo, yet she sees,
la comunicación no existe, but yet we all speak.
Mayra Benítez needs to tell someone,
I feel like I dropped a load off my back.
Adriana Cárdenas has a job: I know I must find it.
Sergio López knows people know, but this gets him:
We put our hands together and pray for the one that kills,
and blame the innocent. What can stop *la injusticia?*

Death doesn't have a specific body Arizbeth Mendoza writes.
Her sister Fabiola doesn't want to wear a mask or be a *hipócrita.*
Listbet Barragán calls *la muerte el vestido,—*
la acumulación de los siglos que nunca se olvidan.
María Rodríquez says her search is for love.
Eliodoro Escobedo wants to be good with friends and parents.

I am a guide on the journey to Macchu Picchu.
I bind each of us to the journey.
Not everyone makes it, safe passage.
I drive home from Seattle in the dark.
I'm straight, not narrow.

Biatris Mondaca calls it an inspired journey.
I own my life, my actions.
I know that. I can't heal my mother's sadness, money.
I relieve myself with memories.
They write their tag names on buildings.
I see what's in my mind.

Ramiro Jiménez asks forgiveness,

for being the hard little *chavalito*
that used to gang bang for a color.
His friends lost. José Villegas writes,
We are so much stronger. Strong prayer,
raza unida, best old bicycle.

When I feel I'm going down
I run to the stone.
My name, day by day, is Graciela Verdusco.
Hi homies, I have been crossing the river
with you guys. Ramiro,
that's the sweetest line.

On another day a young woman asks, *Mr. Bodeen,*
you know what a coyote is? Well, my father
was a coyote. He was the best coyote.
All the Mexicans wanted to cross with him.
Nadia Valdovinos puts up all her thoughts.
I see me, who said I couldn't. I left you awhile back.
José Lozano comes in to talk about the *barranca.*
El cielo siempre está limpio.
Israel Ceja travels for his thoughts.
José Covarrubias for his dead father.
Seven years ago I became the man of the house.
Nobody thought I cared because I didn't cry.
Marta Huerta for pecados y culpa como cadenas.
Rosa Muñiz for the questions.
Yoshimi Varela, sister of Alma,
for the journey with her sister.
She writes from a blue place.
The blue place becomes a *desaparecido.*
Am I odd? I walk the vereda each day.
Es mi camino. Alfredo Barriga
exclaims, *tan hermoso!*
David Gutiérrez, Aztec soul, wipes away a name.
He asks, Tell me your secrets, show me your skill.
He writes to the father who left.
We are discovering America.
Each word will be the final word, the new beginning.
Each word breaks an abstraction.
Each word acts from devotion.
Devotion breaks the trail laid down by belief.

October 1-31, 1996
Day of the Dead/Día de los Muertos
Yakima-Turtle Island

✦

A POEM FOR THE NEW OFFICE

—for Janeen

The baker's with his dog.
Lacy, you have beautiful eyes.
The puppy makes me practice, and I am the puppy.
Baking for two days is good for the soul,
but I have to find a recipe that lets the mind drift.
Candy is too precise. My divinity caramelizes.
I pour it onto wax paper as peanut brittle.
Dreams from the past two nights confuse me.
Last night a man tells me about a house to rent.
I've already lived in it, I know this house,
but say nothing. Driving me to it,
he pulls up next to a covered wagon parked on a ranch.
All I have to do here is dream.
Start your day as many times as you need to.
Russian tea cakes give me the repetition
I'm looking for. My friend makes these.
I'm still being pulled in two directions.
The pup at my feet wants to play.
The office is a spiritual center.
This is the new world. Surround myself with me.
When I turned into my dreams I knew
I had left everyone behind. Everyone.
Lacy Dreamwalker, the black lab at my feet,
is the most common dog bred in this valley.
My friends say it's a shame she can't hunt.
Letting one's children go is a conversion, too.
No one understands. During the epic battle
during the longest night, I find myself
in a large, cold warehouse, attacked
by European armies I can't identify.
I am defenseless, but defended from behind
by protectors I never see. Tracking my dream

on solstice takes most of the night. From
2: 44 on, I take notes. Frightened all the time,
I become confident in my defense, not me.
In this adventure of my life I call for help
in the external world, the kitchen where
I mold the Russian Tea Cakes in my hand.
Bullets of butter and sugar.
Cannon balls aimed at the heart.
Let others cling to shame if they need it.
My pup is a retriever of dreams.
The dream that kicks my ass protects me.

Love, Jim

•

So this is what it's like to be king. Merry Christmas.
Receive what's been given. I've been given skis.
Like Joseph. Dreamer turned bureaucrat,
Joseph provides. Giving and receiving
is the same thing. I have new skis for Christmas.
From my son and the family. Don't reason need.
They need to give. I need to receive.
Inner work in this house. Rewiring
the family code, leaving it exposed,
a kind of charm. Christmas giving begins
with dreams. Karen wakes
after a dream with her father
while I get a friendly volleyball game.
Dream work. A personal autograph
by Steve Mahre crosses my left ski.
I understand my tears for Karen's dream.
I do not understand the dream.
God must want me to ski.

Grandma Myra began this devotion to giving
in 1938 when she took her handsome husband
from the frozen plains of North Dakota
to the sanitarium in Minnesota because of syphilis.
Seeds of change. I had the seed story but I couldn't
track it to me until I read Mom's Reflections,
the story of her life she gave the family this Christmas.

Thinking like a seed. Dear Gardener,
growing organic seeds requires devotion,
hard work and close adherence to nature's timing.
Mother knew I had what I needed to crack the code,
she couldn't talk while we were opening gifts.
Read the story, she said, We'll talk after Christmas.

This is the small story, not the grand one.
Theologians who trace Christ's crucified body to wild dogs
do not witness to the poem. Lost bones rattle inside song lines.
Great giving. Devotion. Fight and light.
Grandma Myra became her bread.
Do not believe the small story of your family.
Do not believe great giving traces itself to a virus.
Believe the praise.
Believe the praise is the response to life.
Believe the point in time when this family first gave thanks.
Believe that *thank you* is true response.

It crosses my mind, dozing, putting James Hillman's
Soul Code on my forehead,
that I'm reading charged words on bad seed,
his essay on Hitler; and when woken
by my daughter stuck in the ice, I'm pulled sweating
from murder and evil. That's all I know,
the driving animal is the terrible fear
of being inadequate to the demanding vision of the daiman.
Hillman, the great oak, spirit father,
dropping word seeds, wise tall tree
with the curious, devotional, potent imagination,
connecting above and below, urging us to freedom,
Hillman, calling on me in my house,
in the early dark hours, from his carefully
built chapter on evil, ripping me from sleep,
a guiding image. Hearing this may not be easy.

And I get up with the dog,
descending the stairs, finding this,
It takes a large heart to accept a tight collar.
Fear of finding myself evil drives me to the middle,
but the middle, too, is a divine path. *The truer*
you are to your daiman, the closer you are to your death

that belongs to your destiny. I am a dead man walking.
I've said so. I feel. My life from this seed.
Called to life and honesty. Called from self-control,
from denial and innocence and even belief,
to a messier, less certain, way. To the bush soul.

Even here, guided by this morning,
I discover myself, driven, not quite present
to the dream. Last night at the movies with Karen,
the popcorn, so good because it's not holiday sacred.
The movie, made from a novel by the poet,
Michael Ondaatje, takes me, by story, into my life.
I find myself thinking of this poem, believing I could write
myself clean every morning.
What I see on the screen is daily life lived in love
that comes from neither good or bad circumstances.
Popcorn is neither fudge nor divinity.
Before my eyes, only the story.
I take what is given. I receive it.
If I'm given skis, I ski. If I'm given dream, I dream.
The nurse keeps the man alive because she is a nurse.
She keeps him alive until he gives up his story.
The story is set in an old monastery. The piano is wired
to a bomb by the departing army.

When I hear the story I know I am alive.
When Karen tells me her dream I know
what I have been given. Twenty-eight years ago
in a basement apartment during the first year of marriage,
making love, I remember Karen's first orgasm,
and me thinking, Now I am a lover.
I had the clitoris, I did not have the story.
I took the fragments of her story,
gave her, her mother, in her mother's voice,
talking to her for the first time, gave it to her.
I made her story up, and made it mine.
Still, she hadn't told it herself. She hadn't given it up,
in her words, willingly. I had to wait
until I had given up. She had to do her own work.
The quiet woman enters the room, *I nearly forgot,*
I had this dream, I was in this secret room, upstairs.
It's a place where I could go, nobody knew about it but me.

The clitoris does its work. It surfaces for joy
in order to protect the dream. The dream is where
the woman goes to find herself.

Invent a truer illusion, where fable dominates,
I will not let what is true and strange be put
in a world of facts. Wordsworth works on The Prelude
his entire adult life, and makes two poems,
the poem of 1805, and the poem of 1850.
A traveler I am, whose tale is only of his life.
I want to chart the lives.
Every voice, every story gathered in one place.
First Sergeant Tommy Pendergrass, West Texas Irish Baptist,
mentors the young private in Panama. I am 20 years old.
He has a snapshot of himself by Hemingway's grave.
We read Donleavy's Ginger Man,
drive the Panama-American Highway home,
gringos coming to Oaxaca from the South.
He flies to Seattle to meet my family, to take their son to Viet Nam.
I don't want Tommy Pendergrass lost in a misplaced poem,
I want Pendergrass here with me.

Frank Malgesini, son of Italian and Irish immigrants
who settled in the Yakima Valley, my infuriatingly
loyal friend, lives, teaches and translates
in Mexico, raising a family, also charmed, as if in exile,
twenty years after his vision to teach Mexican kids
in our Valley proved to be too successful to be believed.
Frank Malgesini, son of Frank Malgesini,
taught the Quixote, all 1000 pages of it to students
who weren't supposed to be able to read.
And when the dust had cleared he left for Morelia,
Guadalajara, Chihuahua, Mexico D. F.,
the Pyramids of the Sun and Moon,
and learning Spanish and creating visions for all schools,
does again what he did in Yakima Valley,
teaching the great books with a larger vision,
alabanza, and he shows up one day in my back yard
and shows me my poems of my family's dispersal,
and my father's death, translated into Spanish,
alabanza, my own mother talking to her grandchildren
in a language she never herself spoke.

Frank Malgesini, teacher, translator, husband,
casting himself into a world with no guarantees,
no illusions, except in words made to stand in wind.

There is a seizure. Denial and innocence.
Blind in one eye and paralyzed on one side
of the body. Denial and innocence. Karen thinks
it's the Gulf War. She's wrong on this one.
Five months later I am in Chile,
chosen by a group of economists to witness
to the new economy. At first no one knows
about the poetry. We are in Mapuche country.
The *machi* speaks directly to me.
I breathe his smoke. I carry Neruda
with me at all times, from *La Chascona,*
his house in Santiago, to the retreat at Isla Negra.
I am holding Neruda's poems when Pinochet
enters the bookstore surrounding us
with his officers and their Uzis.
I offer my free hand.
I witness to the fence poles surrounding Isla Negra.
I call the poles sentries.
I carve the words given to me.
The machi gives me everything.
To be a *machi* you have to die.
I am sHADOWmARKED.

I print business cards that mean business,
The business of literature.
Take a bullet, make a song.
Crazy Horse speaks to me through Mari Sandoz.
Denial and innocence.
I send my son away. I take him from his mother,
send him into the wilderness. He goes willingly, on his own.
I pronounce my life over.
I stay in a monastery and give my son to God.
I drive to Pine Ridge.
I give all I have left at Black Elk's stone.
Denial and innocence.
I try not to carry anything that is not mine.
I honk at the car with the bumper sticker that reads
Straight but not narrow.

In the shower this morning,
it is Don Eduardo's voice, the *machi*,
And how is the Red Man in your country?

Discipline. Always discipline.
Without discipline I couldn't get to the poem.
The day Karen became a bank officer
I took over the kitchen, the voice under my breath,
I'm no outdoor barbecue cook.
Today I'm a baker. I learned patience
making wine. When I emptied the alcohol
from this house, I took bottles of Pinot Noir,
Cabernet Sauvignon, Chardonney, pressed
with my hands and bottled in oak, corked,
laid on their side to wait for me. And blackberries
picked from my father-in-law's. Aged
for as long as fifteen years, I took them to the garbage dump
and broke them one at a time, broken spirits
mirroring my broken life.
I couldn't see the discipline
until I cleared the spirit.
Trying to become the bread.
A legacy to my children.

It has snowed 14 inches by 6 am and coming down.
Karen is in Ellensburg with our daughters,
helping them take those great small steps
into their own story. Lacy wakes twice in the night
missing Karen, hops on the bed looking for her.
I am listening to music from 500 nations, a musical journey,
thinking of these twin daughters, in their struggle
to separate, from each other, from parents.
An Eskimo shaman in a TV movie advises me,
Find many ways to say nothing.
Leah packs for Morelia. Krista holds up her fingers,
showing me two twos. She is 22.
The only thing for certain is my mother's voice.
She tells me Krista reminds her of her.
I recall lines saved in praise,
yet being unable to listen on the telephone.
Women in my life tear at my face.
Shish kabob sticks, protruding from opposite ends,

offering different fruits. I feel them with my fingers.
One daughter, called to the world in cosmic innocence.
One daughter, called by the angel of perfection.
Both called to teach.
Krista works three jobs, grave yard waitress in a truck stop,
afternoons in a day care, weekends in sales at J. C. Penneys.
She works her classes around her jobs.
Leah knows every class she'll take for the next two years.
She knows what she needs to learn in Mexico.
She's a swim team coach and she carries a stop watch.
She doesn't speak Spanish, but she has a plan.
She tells me not to worry. I say I'm being a father.
I say, Brush your teeth.
She says, I do, five times a day.
Karen comes through the door with a new haircut.
I say, Let me see. I like it. Do you like it?
She sees the shish kabob sticks in my face.
She's not fooled by my attention.
She sees the contortion caused by the sticks
pulling from the lower chin to the opposite cheek.
She sees the pineapple chunk under my eye,
the charred point of the threatening burnt tip.
Her acceptance of the way things are has power.
I'm looking for many ways to say nothing.
She tells me I'm a wreck.
It is not a difficult thing for her to say.
She knows I made this face myself.
This is no movie, she says.
There's no train, no train wreck in the living room.
There's only tonight, and that face.
And you made that face, you made it on your own.

Back from Viet Nam, meeting a man.
A teacher gives me Blake,
and then the Romantics, including Wordsworth's
spots of time, transforming the imagination,
sustaining and transforming the present.
In the teacher's office, itself a World War II Quonset hut,
he shows me Lewis's little book on grief,
and I discover the fragment of his wife's death
giving birth, giving me access to my own trauma,
and beginnings with Lewis. The teacher takes me next door

to another professor, who teaches me Shakespeare
in this little room, a tutorial, the way Lewis taught,
and we talk and read and I write papers
and read them to him, and write them again,
and we do this with Lear four times running.
I am given Heilman's book, This Great Stage,
even then out of print, and we read and cry
and talk, and then I am given Merton
and biography, and when my son is born
I am eating at my teacher's house, my own road before me.
The teacher tells me about the night
his wife dies giving birth, and we are linked,
howling into the night, my teacher and I.

Blake connects me to my own past,
for a line is not formed by chance.
A line is a line in its most minutest subdivisions,
the rural North Dakota Lutheran Church across the street
from the Victorian house the elevator company
furnished for our family. Straight or crooked,
Blake is a bridge to Job and to Merton.
I meet Harald Sigmar, the Lutheran pastor
who knows Lewis, and he gets me
to the Catholics and Vatican II. But I couldn't get to Jesus.
And Christ was an idea. A concept.
(I had found Williams. No ideas. Beautiful thing.)
I am alone with Williams, No ideas but in things.
Asphodel was all women, and I fell in love reading Asphodel
frightened out of my mind, and Karen becomes
my spiritual wife, and I am devoted to her.

Feeling all this, all of the poets singing within me,
still unable to find Jesus, I find the Catholics,
a single course on Jesus but it's not possible.
I have to give three summers, three years.
This is life. Living in community
I'm not prepared for. Priests and nuns.
Because I am outside the tradition
I had to do some things. And because I also belonged
I would be accepted, taken in,
and I would take the blood and body, and Karen would come
and I would take Merton and Lewis and be a seeker.

Poet, husband, father, monk, prophet,
a part of Vatican II, whole, a member,
and I would investigate every question, look behind
each stone, leaving nothing sacred.
Riding on a downtown bus in Seattle my mother
asks me if I still believed like a Christian,
and I ask her back, What do Christians believe?
I found the teachers who gave me all,
the new criticism demythologizing Jesus.
And Stanley Marrow gives me Bultmann,
demythologizing Lewis: *Jim, what's the matter?*
Compared to Bultmann, Lewis is an ant.
I remember when the last question fell.
Neither Lewis or Bultmann. Everything else.
I remember my euphoria. *I am nothing.*
Response to what has been given is all.
But this is about denial. My degree, bound
in the red leather of the Cardinals,
does not confer on me a community.
And I take my new knowledge back to the world
alone and I remain alone.
And everything that I know remains in my head,
Crossan, Bultmann, Kung, Tillich, Lewis,
and I lock it up in arrogance and anger,
a Lutheran in a Catholic world, a Catholic in a Lutheran world,
a poet in my own world, working alone
outside the world of poetry,
and it feeds on itself for fifteen years.

And I am given the seizure because I asked for it.
When I wake up it is all there breaking free
in a free fall into the heart, younger, descending joy,
guides everywhere led by Dante and Virgil,
descending with the visual poet to the darkest regions,
where the eye can see no more, and here,
at this low point, turning back, ascending,
hearing something more, and carrying this
back with me, *the ear knows things the eye*
can only guess at. Everything,
everything I'd been given, carried this time
by Rilke, Vatican II, Orpheus,
new life in the surrounding wreckage, and

even in this newly fossilized world, more work to do.

And still not to the dream work.

✦

SNOWFALL FOR KAREN

May the words in this letter fall freely
for whoever knocks to enter this house.
May the words fall like the snow,
may they break the form of fathers
writing letters to daughters.
You are born finding your place
and your calling will not go away.
The sound of the flute moves me through time.
Williams said everything to Flossie in Asphodel,
maybe everything to all women, say it again.

The snow lady stands across the room
dressed to go out, her green wool scarf wrapped
tight under her snow chin, her cuffs pulled tight
around her white wrists. Three bears
in a rocking chair sit at my right elbow.
Grandpa Bear's wearing spectacles,
dressed in his knickers and sweater,
wearing his apron full of more working tools
than I own. His string Beard's a cave
for the little one rocking in his arms,
too young for clothes except for the red ribbon.
Candles and bears. Signs of Karen surround me.

Karen's at work. The bonsai finca,
an anniversary gift from Karen two years ago,
can be seen again with Christmas decorations taken down.
A dozen bears rest under three remaining poinsettias.
Two old monks sit on a bench under the spreading limbs.
Walking with Karen in Eugene this fall
we pass a group of dancing Krishnas led by a man
about my age. I try to see myself in his smile.
There is something missing
that's never missing in me when I'm empty.

He isn't surrounded by Karen.
One of the monks in this living room is me.

Calls come in for Karen. They wake the pup.
I look to the little bottles on the mantle.
Cut glass and mirrors. All the ways I look for Karen.
Janeen can't believe she has to work on her birthday.
She'll call the bank from her cell phone.
Bob calls from Hawaii. He has her 800 number.
He laughs. Cut glass and Karen.
One of the hot scents in perfume is grapefruit.
One of my favorite fruits.
Fragrance creations. Citrus notes of mandarin.
Luscious heart notes of rose.
From this house, one of the ways Karen
goes into the world is in perfume.

•

The battle for this house takes place on all fronts.
My dad drives us off a dangerous pass in the dream world.
We are evacuating students from Elsinore,
having just seen Hamlet. My father is driving
children to their freedom.
He has returned to me in dreams as my father.
Stopped at a roadblock, Dad clears the way
and I drive. We have joined with the actors.
Taking people to freedom. Waking
to write the dream, I know the fight
with snow and water isn't over. New Year's Eve,
and two feet of snow on the roof. Snow
turning to hard rain. The house under siege.
I shovel snow to release the water as the rain hits.
Water and ice flood the gutters. I build snow dikes
on both sides of the house during the dying light.
Toy dams under a deluge.
Dream images in the external world.
Karen cuts me plastic to cover the snow.
The margin that keeps this house dry, less than two inches.
On the roof, in the basement, we are safe.
I talk with a woman in the dream
about the numbing effects of poverty on children.

She says she didn't know.
Malnourished children don't learn.
I'm proud of my dad. Returned to me
in the inner world, he helps me under siege
in the outer world. Upstairs, downstairs.
This sentence in this house.
çompleting itself for 25 years.
I knew nothing when I came here.
Inside, outside.
A beginner in the dream field.

Rolling Karen's poem in a flower vase,
I take it to her at the bank.
I carry cut flowers from Safeway.
She likes the poem so much she wants to show it around.
It's not the poem. It's the snow lady in the poem.
One of the women at the bank made the snow lady.
But the poem has stuff in it that can't be released.
Karen takes out the second stanza.
Karen becomes an editor.
Karen takes herself out of the poem
to become the dream image.

If process is God, this is process.

It feels like Monday, she says with orange juice.
Two days of work, two days off. We're going to give
monthly bonuses. We want people starting out
to know they have a chance. First day of work
in the new year, January 2. Bank with Karen.
It's my birthday, Karen says. *The book we're reading,*
may be too much—seven ways
to God may be more than some want.

This poem gets up in the morning and writes itself.
Exploring liminal time, the poem asks for more.
It turns itself inside out.
My father turns out to be my father.
Dad, Oh, Dad.
You were my father all along.
A plane flies over the house.
I make a list before turning out the light.

New Year. Snow. Barry/Conversation. Dreams.
Barry comes by as I write these lines.
He has been at the library,
tells me about a book of poems,
What we don't know about each other.

•

The blizzard gives me time to clear my head.
Barry and I talk poetry for 20 years.
A forged conversation under the influence
of the great themes and the salmon of knowledge.
A line is itself,
not intermeasurable by anything else.
From the line direct to the line meandering.
From the edited poem to the impulse of the heartbeat.
Twenty years of letter poems.
Twenty years of notebooks.
Twenty years. A working school. A conversation.
Beginning with the inheritance: *Beautiful thing.*
And the ancestors: *Who's there?*
Beginning with a line that becomes a creed:
The yakima is on the yakima. The yakima empties into the Columbia.
To the coded glance.
A haiku poet stops the rain from coming in
by moving a single board.
Much of what we accomplish in talk
made possible through thunder and rain.
The poet of the eye. The poet of the ear.
At the threshold, then, two men
talk poetry every day.
One doesn't bother with roofs leaking,
when the poem is primary.
When the poem is primary
it is not only lovers who find each other.

•

The job last night is to choose a new pope.
Tradition doesn't need an election for transfer of power.
Tradition can wait for the old pope to die.
Nature has more freedom. It does what it does.

The dream will never submit to a vote.
Whose vote? And whose interpretation?
Baking with Julia is more than a cookbook.
But you can't learn to knead by following directions.
Your super mixer can peak a meringue,
but it can't help you fold it into boiling syrup.
The job of the morning can't be seen.
My daughters. Separating from each other.
When one of them enters the room
I must answer in my own voice.
Listening, I must not understand.
Listen when they call.

•

ANGEL TALK

—for Leah

The letter must be the first sign of the angel.
The voice that calls us to talk
really asks us to be ourselves.
You were really singing last night.
I don't believe in God, but I believe in angels.
What you call the angel, I call the dream.
That talk last night—let me be clear about this;
It wasn't between a father and daughter.
That was a conversation with the angels.
Letters must be the demands of our angels.
They won't let us be anyone but ourselves.
When you listen to yourself, doesn't it change everything?
When you changed universities
maybe you were really being called by a voice
you had to follow but didn't understand.
Now you can see. It's your angel.
You gave up something big to discover another part of you.
Friday you fly to Morelia, Michoacán.
It has nothing to do with airplanes.
You're traveling into yourself.
Your letter and talk last night is proof.
You have made the invisible world visible.
This is dream work, what angels do.

Last night you took out the losses of the past.
You found the bullet behind the bullet.
We need to know where we've been hit.
When we know we're no longer innocent
we don't have to carry any guilt.
People walk around not knowing they're bleeding.
Aren't they the real innocents?
The bullet behind the bullet
really comes from the angel.
This is the sacred bullet.
You've found it. Make a song.
Your angel wants you to belong to yourself.
Look at everything.
Leave behind anything you don't need.
Your angel will never leave you.
When you return in March, call.

•

This morning, the last morning of the holidays,
I fall asleep writing the letter.
I ask Karen for the date of Thanksgiving.
The question makes no sense to her.
Our 28th Anniversary, November 23.
It began then. *When did the poem change,*
and tumble into this house? 44 days.
44 mornings. Lines don't begin to tell.
Ulysses tackles 24 hours. One morning.
I turn into myself on the couch.
My coffee is cold. I want to tell Karen.

For 44 days I have not held back.
I gave everything I had.
I didn't get it all done.
The day waits for anyone.
Krista's the last to leave.
She takes the cat with her
returning to school.
I say to Karen, 44 days.
From our Anniversary to now.
How'd I do?
Overall? she asks.

Overall, I'd give you A-.
A-.
44 days.
I don't have the energy to put the dog down.
Abolish grades in all schools, forever.

Give myself fifteen minutes.
Look at these lines from yesterday.
I went back to Karen working on the sewing machine.
A-. A-. She laughs. Consider the house.
This house still stands.
Snow. Ice. Rain. Water.
Roof. Ceilings. Walls. Basement.
I didn't mention good deeds.
She raises the grade. She laughs.
I asked too soon, I say.
I asked too soon.

I look one time at Karen's gift vest.
Reversible double patterned Pendleton wool.
Northwest Indian on the side with pockets.
Southwest Indian on the inside.
Two pockets display the inside on the outside
along with three wood buttons.
Hand-sewn button holes, and a black border
uniting both worlds.
I am humbled and proud of this work of my wife.
This vest is a house.

The electrician is at it again, rewiring.
It's all practical.
He goes into the corporation itself.
It's simple, but everything will be new.
It's an anniversary for me, too.
The anniversary of the bullet.
Yesterday, Miguel Santana tells me,
Not everyone has to take a bullet.
¿Que es el pasaporte para entrar a dos mundos?
The electrician simply shuts it down.
And he kept an open barrel for burning
anything he didn't want. You see,
I lost something, that's why I'm asking

these questions. Maybe that's the ticket
to enter, the loss of something very great.
You have to lose something to gain,
Pedro Hernandez says. The electrician
simply won't work with the old wiring.
This is no ordinary electrician.
He's giving working men a new code to light our houses.
He makes a point to name his wage, too.
$83,000. Why would the dream give me that one?
How do you know you're in two worlds?
List the worlds you live in, Santana.
Hazme una lista.
Can I call you Santana?
I'm telling you my dream, Santana.
I'm calling you by name.

He wants to know why the story
I'm giving him is in two languages.
Six years ago today I was given a new life.
Now I hardly recognize my friends.
My own wife is one more person to love.
Santana, Cuando la clase empezó,
me preguntaste en inglés, y ahora
me pregúntas en español. ¿Por qué?
¿Cuándo tú estás enojado, cuál idioma prefieres?
Don't make me mad.
¿Cuándo hablas de amor con tu novia, hablas español?
Cierto.
¿Por qué?
Que lenguaje se hablan en tu mundo de sueños?
It's confusing.
Both languages come up in dreams.
You tell me you lost your mother. You want her back.
Once you know you live in two worlds,
once you know, that's where you belong.
You can't be in any other place.
You need that place all the time.
You're neither here nor there.
One world simply doesn't cut it.
It's old wiring. The gang doesn't work anymore.
You can't go back to Mexico.
Los gabachos no entienden nada.

El mundo de los gabachos se acabó.
Un fracaso de shopping malls y televisión.
Our home is another world.
¿Dónde existe este mundo para ti?
En la charla de la historia.
En la confusión del sueño y el cuarto.
Necesitamos literatura ahora.
Yo tengo mi perrita, Lacy Dreamwalker.
She brings me back. She takes me out.
Hits and misses. Between the lines.
Driving to work. Cooking dinner.
The gift of dyslexia.
Between the word and the chord.
Entre la palabra y la música.
Waiting for someone.
Inside. Inside the border itself.
The wilderness is inside.
En medio la frontera existe el mundo salvaje.

On this anniversary of my transportation,
I ask the best students in the United States of America,
Díganme exactamente, ¿qué es como agua para chocolate?
They argue back and forth before Alma says, No,
it's something else. Es algo que está listo,
it's something that's ready to come out, to erupt.
It's neither anger nor algo sexual, but it could be,
and it's more, and it's ready, and when it starts to come
it can't be stopped, it's hot like that. That's como
agua para chocolate, ese.

It's also a book. *Querida Laura Esquivel,*
we have been defending your right to heat the water.
The book first goes down in a blind vote by English teachers.
A librarian calls it smut over the phone.
The curriculum director buries the book.
The Chicana administrator,
boldly refuses to utter one public word.
We follow lessons learned on the way to Macchu Picchu.
Stay cool. Know what you carry in your pack:
Jornada sagrada, lugar sagrado, persona sagrada.
The fundamentalist Christian
voting against the book, asks in tears,

When will it stop? Where will it end? When is enough enough?

This morning we pass out the books.
In Spanish and English.
Our great ganas come from our hunger.
Tita, 15, on the seventh page of the novel, *por*
primera vez en su vida intentó protestar
a un mandato de su madre. Breaking silence.
She wanted to know who started this family tradition.
Once we start down this road.
Once the questions start coming.
What futures? For who?
Dicen que al buen entendedor pocas palabras...
We listen to a taped recording in Spanish,
following in our books.
Hagamos algunos resúmenes en capítulo uno.
We listen to a taped recording in English,
following in our books.
We note differences in the two recordings,
the original text and the translation.
Four experiences not counting our own.
How many do we have?
One hundred minute class period. We're exhausted.
I get to do this twice today. *This day.*
You don't have to think about love.
Orpheus in moonlight.
The hits are only voice lessons.

This is the hidden life of dogs.
What dogs want is to live like wolves.
Elizabeth Marshall Thomas believes dogs are slaves.
We are helpless puppies in your presence.
The odors dogs carry home are daily newspapers
telling other dogs the stories of where they've been.
Sniffing is one way of getting today's news.
Dogs want to belong. Loss of another is big stuff.
Dogs make us ask what we mean to each other.
Dogs in a den don't think about their owners.
A dog's life absorbs itself. People fade.
There is nothing to see.
When dogs are serene they do nothing.
Thomas sits with the dogs in the afternoon dust.

With dogs, Thomas writes, death and odor
go together, not as corruption, but memory.

Lacy and I smell the dead flesh
of the packing plant driving through Ellensburg.
It is early. Strains of Benny Goodman.
Lacy is given music every morning of her life.
We drive in a heated cab through snow and ice
listening to music.
Neither hope or hopelessness.
Two dogs on a morning run.
Driving by the packing plant
I project nothing on the dog.
I am not given what she is given.
I don't smell what she smells.

The dream world works like this.
I throw the pup the tennis ball.
She catches it and puts it at my feet.
She made this game so she could have some fun.
So we didn't have to work all the time.
I come into the kitchen too tired to write it down.
The dream. It got away from me. I change the music.
This is no Chelsea morning, Joni Mitchell.
How many women have written you poems?
How many men have made promises listening to your song?
Night prizes. I'm a proud puppy.

The Old Testament professor has shown up again.
He's a good guy, but I'm tired of him in my dreams.
And he's tired, too, in this one.
All his exams are thrown into the trash.
The Waterman, quiet the entire hour, says one thing,
The professor, too, is waiting to be delivered.
His words come back with the pup and the ball.
That impatient professor isn't in Chicago.
He's in me. He is me. Anxious for destiny.
He's as tired of sociology as I am.
I'm in the kitchen when the dream opens.
Another restaurant dream. I write it down.
The pup barks. She wants my attention.

Alma doesn't want to continue being like.
Seeing Rosario Castellanos face to face,
She didn't eat her anger. ¡Grandiosa Mujer!
One can really be lonely.
One can really be true and free.
I watch as Alma and Yoshimi, linked to me
by a destiny I don't understand, outgrow
their family, their creed, their nation.
Sisters as similar as my identical twin daughters,
and as different. I underline Yoshimi's words,
She forgot the past. She owns her own life,
saying, *I was born from the dream.*
We discover ourselves individually.

In the oldest tradition of Jazz, J. J. Johnson
speaks through his horn. He tells a story.
The more deliberate I am in each act
the more the act belongs to me.
Making biscotti, the twice-baked cookie,
I reconnect to myself in the oven.
Sunday morning.
There will never be another you.
Biscotti for Karen. Music for Ben.
Merle Haggard discovers Iris DeMent.
Making music in the kitchen is like this.
DeMent thanks Haggard for lessons
she can't get anywhere else.
She sings Big City.
A voice goes inside another voice.
When her morning comes around
she won't worry about what she's saying.
In the wasteland of the free
she'll take her sorrow straight.
Making each cup of coffee makes each one mine.
J. J. is no tailgater. His songs all go to Vivian.
Dear Karen, there is no place I do not go.

I have moved into the kitchen.
I knew and didn't. Emptying the dishwasher
gives me a place to work.

•

FOOTNOTES

That's what I thought they'd look like, Barry says
when I show him the lines on counting.
Making time count. That's one line I wanted in
and left out. Barry asks for days in the title,
Counting Days. *3 days with no food but rosebuds,*
Pound writes in Canto 89. The footnotes want to take
the story further. Barry says they're for the reader
in The Atlantic Monthly. I don't want a maze—
footnotes are in the poems and notebooks.
They're on my walls. They're in the garden.
They're in the cookbooks in the kitchen.
The rumor went about that Pound had abandoned words,
Kenner writes in The Pound Era. He was 62
when he met Pound. *El duende* is the goblin wind
behind a person's creative life. Addiction
is anything that depletes life while making
it appear better. Pound was 82. *What habit*
merely retains, art will remember. Kenner's point
is that Pound had no one tracking his trail.
Renaissance of attention! He had the freedom
of a poem which he owned and operated.

One day I woke up. Kenner's great book remains.
Metamorphosis—identity persisting through change.
I have thought for some time, that the seizure
didn't just happen. God didn't just choose me,
I had to prepare for it. Kenner roused me
from the beginning, perhaps entering me
ten years before I was called.
Seed change for the gestalt?
Counting days became a way to move towards now.
Betrayals occur when those who have power
see trouble and look away. Dante heard something deeper
when he could see no more. Being on the mountain
is not all switch backs. Looking at those numbers
this morning. Call it dreaming.

•

BACK TO THE ONE

My friend wants access for the outside world.
Because the language has been politicized
it isn't free to carry the experience.
We don't believe in God because
he hasn't seized us yet. But I have been seized.
Counting days is a stone cold experience.
I'm stoned right now.
In ecstasy, wrapped up in days.
But the language is held captive in the village.
We live in a world that doesn't understand symbol.
Neither poets or drunks.
I am listening to Aaron Neville sing.
A bottle of liquor shows up in a dream.
People think it must be about alcohol.
I have just taken cookies from the oven.
What bubbles up within me must be part of the quest.
Love calls with all that's in you.
These are impersonal principles.
The symbol is the manifestation of something invisible in me.
These cookies on the counter.
They're not the same cookies that went into the oven.
The days have nothing to do with sobriety.
Just the opposite, and beyond.
I'm walking around drunk.
Dreams aren't sent to gussie up our lives.
Counting days is music, ecstatic breath.

•

A photo of Garcia Márquez and Neruda shows up my mail.
They're in France admiring a sculpted naked breast.
I am a visionary of days, fundamentalist in nothing.
Márquez has his hand on the ivory thigh.
He enjoys this moment more than Neruda.
I have moved into the kitchen.
I knew and didn't know
what the room had become.
Cleaning the sink gives me a place to work.

It started like that.
I have the pup. There is the oven.
Flour, water, salt and yeast.
Learn to knead. Become the bread.
I go over this real slow with Karen.

Worship of Dionysos will never be explained.
Orpheus, I promise everything.
Let me be open to the energies.

✦

PRIVATE MYSTERY, PUBLIC RITUAL

"For the inspiration of the moon comes, the myths relate,
from the dark moon and from the soma drink brewed from the moon tree."
—M. Esther Harding

I am an initiate in the female mysteries.
If the true husband is the moon
it doesn't matter who you marry.
There is a man in the moon, too.
These are impersonal principles.
Listen to the woman:
I had an emotional reaction
to your note, like when we hold hands
at the end of the meeting in A.A.
I look around at the faces
of other redeemed people
and get a wash of love.
Listen to the man:
The hopes and fears of the ordinary man
is a problem. The cry of the Orphics
is a cry in the wilderness. Orphic
catharsis is an elaborate system of rules
observed continuously. Nothing less
than purity is demanded.
Essential divinity.
Constant, ritual purity.
Ekstasis, enthusiasm, deep spiritual hope.
Listen to the woman:
I get really filled up for that moment.

You look so happy with your beautiful dog.
I wanted to keep on. I got clubbed
over the head with love.
Listen to the principle:
About the soma it is said:
...the moon.
That is Soma, the king.
They are food of the gods.
The gods do eat it.
Having reached the moon they become food.
Man, too, can participate. Atman.
Through this ritual, within the worshiper,
a self, not personal ego, divine,
free of all pairs of opposites—
never bending the head to anyone,
develops in that individual who undergoes
the required initiations to the moon deity.
The ritual of the soma drink accesses god,
losing personal, conscious control, prey
to the great whatever within.
The great playground!
Thoughts and inspirations.

What is going on health-wise?
I am now seeing a naturopath
for that goddamn Chronic Fatigue Syndrome—
I'm not mellow on this topic.
I am on this allergy elimination deal
which ferrets out hidden
food and substance allergies.
Treatment, and detoxing from whatever
doesn't agree with you.
I got very stuck in detoxing
from Vitamin C. I know—
sounds weird—there's all those heavy duty
detoxes like heroin and crack,
and here I am
thrashing around with Vitamin C.
The doctor had me on one bland food, oatmeal.

I went to see him today,
cussing like crazy,

as I said, not mellow.
It turns out I am very allergic
to the gluten in oatmeal.
It turns out I'm also allergic to wheat.
It boggles my mind, seeking answers
from doctors for years
and no one could get humble—
Gee maybe it's the oatmeal.
I haven't had the heart
to look in my Roethke book.
I will go to the ends of the earth
to get well. I'm sure telling
you a lot of stuff.
Did you and Karen
see that moon on Christmas Eve?

Unveiled by custom
lines build a path
that can be followed, going forward,
following children,
the instincts of the dog.
This is the language of the godly.
Wisdom that knows
without knowing how.
Soma is the moon drink,
making itself.

•

PRICELESS GIFT

Moon drink, Soma.
Cauldron of inspiration.
Moon's gift.
Inspiration, ecstasy, leading to the final initiation.
But not from the mind, from the dark moon.
From the Soma, brewed from the Moon Tree.
Not in thought. Dark obscure movements.
Impulses of darkness.
To create, make that which wasn't.
The moon is Soma.

Those who take it, giving,
become dust, turn to smoke,
and then to night. Having reached,
they become food.
Thinking about him, become him.

Homeless initiation,
not dependent, not conditioned.
Daring to listen to the inspiration within.
And required, under the requirements
of feminine principles. Soma.
Losing conscious control.
Drinking— the initiate is filled with the god.
Prey to whatever from the unknown,
thought or inspiration.
Renouncing self-control.
Surrendering to the impulse,
the ecstasy of the strange.
Laying aside personal autonomy.
Great act of devotion.
Giving himself up.
Resigned to the dark powers.
Inner spark speaking on its own,
No creed, no belief.

Not wide knowledge, not erudition.
Nature that knows without knowing how.
Using everything that comes.
What birds know.
And fantasies, intuitions.
Intoxicating delights coming and going
on their own, demanding outlet,
uncensored,
giving one thing, renewal,
through partaking,
disinterested,
towards one's depths, one's limits.
A path of redemption through things
which are the lowest.

✦

Between Lacy and Karen.
Karen whistling and snorting.
Lacy's stomach coming up.
I put my arm around Karen.
She says, Let me sleep.
Lacy eats her vomit.
I rise to discover new snow.
I make each cup of coffee
the way the monks teach me
to light candles. Feel the energies
in this house, this January morning.

What are we trying to get out of, I ask.
There's a man and a woman
sitting on a rock.
Joni Mitchell sings
to the mystical husband.
Freezing rain falls
over an inch of snow.
Starting my truck
Coltrane's blowing hard,
way out, way out in front of us.

✦

SOMA ON THE MOUNTAIN

Soma is all there is.
Standing above tree line at White Pass.
This is the Soma of the moment.
Even the weather is between rain and snow.
Skiing with my son and daughter-in-law
between the already and the not-yet.
Twenty years ago I said to myself,
Maybe someday. What I called dreams.
Last night puppies turned into boys
playing basketball.

White boys in the parking lot at the mountain pass
play city music, black street talk traveling for miles.

I ask these boys, *Do you think these lyrics*
might be obscenities or invasions?
They tell me it's a free country.
It's just music.
I carry my anger up the mountain.
I try to explain Soma to my son.
No before, no after.
Only what comes up.
Born on this mountain,
and born again in the wilderness,
my son knows these trails better than he knows himself.
My anger comes up from another drainage.
My skis turn towards a patch of blue sky
where a cloud moves in.
Waiting to ride the lift I make a big deal of my new skis.
My son and his wife bought me these skis.
An extravagance systemic in our family.
See that personal autograph by the Olympic skier?
Putting on my new coat before leaving the house
I ask my wife if she can still see me,
if it's possible to see anything but this jacket shine.
These K-2's go where there are no trails.
This is me waiting for the ski lift.
The moon shines and the ocean churns.
Stir it up, Bob Marley sings, Stir it up.
This is the cosmic must from the ocean's cup
that never empties, this is the drink
that just keeps coming.
Walking into the lodge with our lunches,
I discover I'm missing a glove.
A friend of my son's hollers at me.
I ingratiate myself. I feel foolish,
wondering who I am in all these shiny clothes.

All day to myself. All day.
Soma keeps right on running.
It is the rekindling of the dream
and the dream's destruction.
It is the hot wax between the ski and the snow.
My skis tracking the now.
Through trees, on moguls.
A small shift of weight makes this possible,

where to end one line, begin a new one.
How to squeeze life into the poem, not out of it.
It is a free fall.
A father's awkwardness
before his son.
The clear, bubbling cup of what is.

✦

CONSIDER THE WATERMAN

Puppies run up and down the ball court
turning into boys, and back into pups.
They're playing basketball.
The white team is behind.
This is my team. I can't tell
if they're puppies or boys.
Trying to distinguish
myself from the culture
I return once more to the well.
The Waterman points to the Phoenix Moon.
He knows a woman who has returned
from the dark side.
Most of the time the ball players are boys.
Me and one other puppy
try to escape from obedience school.
My puppy mimics me perfectly.
I can no longer tell which dream
is from which world.
Driving with my son,
he takes Coltrane from the music box,
saying we'll never arrive if I keep
following that horn.
The Waterman hands me the cup.
I dip it in the well.
Let's see what comes up, he says.
The puppy and I splash in water.
We have forgotten the ball game.
I watch her pee on a book.
All of the pages dissolve in a pool of urine.
A uniformed man chases us in a garden.
The puppy is completely, foolishly, me.

The Waterman calls on the woman
without a moment's hesitation.
She becomes once more
one in herself, facing whatever it may be,
holding the cup before me.

•

Each of us with a box of matches inside,
Esquivel says. Making matches.
This is June in January.
Look for the matches in ourselves.
Marriage is another word owned by the village.
Altered lives require altered states.
There's more passion in a single friendship
than any marriage sanctified by the state.

•

—Lines for Gayle

Consider this house, consider this morning.
I am being held by a poem that begins each morning
with music, as prayer. Capitulo Seis,
Masa para hacer fósforos. Making matches.
Todos nacemos con una caja de cerillos en nuestro interior.
Each of us already to fire up, but we need the breath
of another person to ignite us.
A woman writes *forgiveness*
across a sheet of paper.
She asks questions like Rilke.
Shouldn't we blaze open the way wild poppies do?
I am reading Esther Harding,
one of the Valkyries of the Dream Master.
Lines come from the desert
which will take you into its silence.
In the white cold of winter
a dog named Beau dies of a torqued bowel
at the vet's kennel. *Impersonal principles.*
A woman writes, Pops has somehow,
inch by inch, consumed all my free energy.
The ecstasy which comes from the Soma drink

may blast the human mind.
The music is Modern Jazz Quartet.
Work on new books is slowed by the dream
of the moment, by nocturnal lines.
Given skis at Christmas, I ski.
This, too, is prayer.
Requiem. Losing a child
to the assassin's bullet is much easier
than letting him go
into his own dream. Atman
is the child of the sacred marriage.
My friend leaves his wife and child
to begin the journey of his life.
What need have we of children,
those of us who have ourselves?
I walk out to the porch each morning
and wave goodby. Feel the certainty
in these lines, wavering
only under the influence of the music.
I am a friend of the wife, too.
Praise mornings, and altered states.
I am being left behind
so that I might better become myself.
I helped cut this trail.
Listen to the Golden Striker.

•

A young woman writes in her notebook:
I have an opinion. I know I have a head to use
and a mouth to express what my anger asks for.
I hate reality. And I am so realistic.
Her older sister writes on the same day:
There is always something that tries
to block your way, that's why
we should fight against everything,
even our morals. *¡Sí niña, pero 'orita pa' qué*
quiero más agrura, si con el mole tengo!
These are political lines.
Javier Vargas reads his poem to the town.
His Macchu Picchu poem wins First Place.
He represents us. The village shakes his hand.

I didn't understand that one in Spanish, not a single word.
But I liked it in English. *I liked it but I don't like your voice.*
The man who has forgotten him says,
You could be a writer.
But he has no papers. He will never study in this country.

We just keep writing our poems, and reading them.
I've never been in a restaurant like this, Javier says.
Tell me about women. Tell me about men.
We talk about the suits. We talk about the *machi.*

✦

Kevin, my letter voice.
It's left the letter, gone inside this poem.
It's with the pup.
The pup plays catch with the tennis ball.
But she wants to bring it all back at once.
She's got a new shoe.
She wants to carry the shoe and the ball.
She can't figure out how to do it.
She wants it all.
She holds the shoe in her mouth,
pushes the ball like a soccer player.

Each day is our child to love.

Go to bed with the poem, get up with the poem.

I throw the ball high.
The pup twirls, chases the ball.
I throw the ball again.
The pup twirls.
The pup twirls every time I throw the ball.
The pup thrills herself each time she twirls.

Letters and poems arrive in the mail.

Letters accompany the poems.

Letters bring me the news I long for.
All the news.

All the lives packed into the letters.

Kevin, these lines to you.
Fellow apprentice in lines.
From the voice in the letters.

✦

LINES FOR MY FRIEND

Soft as in a morning sunrise.
May the divorce be like this,
soft as in a morning sunrise,
as you begin the marriage to yourself.
When Achilleus mourned for his friend Patroklos,
his friend came to him in a dream.
The Modern Jazz Quartet goes solo.
In the Final Concert, it's every man for himself.
This is the promise of new music,
Achilleus himself proclaiming,
We shall set our horses free.
I know this about death—
The village mourns the buried man.
The dead man shopping at Safeway goes unnoticed.
Patroklos tells Achilleus, You were not careless
of me when I lived, only in death.
Listen to the vibraphones.
Lionel Hampton sings to P. Heath.
They are becoming Moon Men.
I grimed my face and wailed
when I lost my child.
My friends said, Look,
I saw him dancing Friday night.
This destiny was given
when I was born, to bring the dreams
from two worlds together.
These are really true blues.
We grew up in the blind man's house.
You'll be a better friend to yourself.
I will miss you horribly.
It's Achilleus' dream. Patroklos tells it.
It is given to nobody to interpret.

You've been given things to do.
When it's all over,
put our ashes in the same urn.

✦

This is not just another petting session.
Start by holding your dog's head in your hands.
Look right into her eyes. Breathe with her,
then lead their breathing to a slower level.
I mourn in the kitchen. I cut vegetables,
bake cookies. Right now I favor a chocolate biscotti.
Biscotti's are twice-baked. Twice in the oven,
first as a log, then sliced on their sides.
Animal massage basics require focus and relaxation.
I listen to large doses of Merle Haggard.
Merle is clean, and empty. An American voice.
Consider the cup. He's got leaving to do.
Leaving with the Sin City Blues.
Big City. Walk off. Keep your retirement,
Singing Iris DeMent, bringing her across
a river, Kern River,
not deep, not wide, but mean,
he can still remember, before
there was a Merle. He learned how
in Bakersfield. He did a little time.
They made him Man of the Year. He picked cotton,
he picked guitar, he danced on Beer Can Hill.
Kern River. He lost his best friend.
Mourn everything. Patroklos. Achilleus.
My daughters ask, *Where will he live?*
Merle sings, kids have bad days, too.
I'm twice baked.
Life and death in every moment.
My friend and I.
We grew up in the house of Homer.
Talked poetry as we made it.
Talked the line.
The colloquial voice, the lyric voice.
Twenty years at this kitchen table.
There.
My friend's word.

He's there.
Our friend from the Gap says,
You fill the gap. You're there.
I tell my friend,
You don't have to fill the gap.
You're there. You're not there.
Take the pizza from the oven.
Turn up the heat.

✦

MORNING LINES FOR JUDY

Dark wings brush against my face.
My cheeks flush.
Bring the dog to your level of breathing.
I am thankful for the mail.
Slow her down, the masseuse says,
let your breath be felt.
Stay focused, and relaxed.
Every dream can be considered a letter
sent to Egypt to awaken us.
I never confuse letters with telephones.
Sometimes I confuse letters with the world.
One problem with the quest is perfection.
When I open the envelope
out pops the critic.
Don't look in your dog's eyes
when you're angry.
The critic wants to have it out.
He wants to know why he hasn't
been shown the poem.
I am being instructed to love my inner enemy.
The critic wants a relationship with me.
I'm in a roomful of women rubbing up
their dogs, the only man.
My black lab is a wild puppy.
A dream retriever. Lacy.
The critic is the next piece of me
asking to be heard.
I ask for this marriage.
I may not be able to read the letter,

but it better be read.
Jesus says,
Many stand outside at the door,
but only the solitaries
enter the bridal chamber.

•

CONSIDER THE BIRTHDAY

—lines for Tom

as another way of leaving,
another way to go.
Pick up the cup in your hands.
Commune with yourself.
The one I care about is my own.
This makes love possible.
With his wine Dionysus is ambivalent.
Inspiration and ecstasy.
Drunk with the blood of Christ,
ecclesiastics raze cities.
Why are their vestments red?
In our birthdays we are fountains
brimming with vital juices.
It is the excess of abstinence I love.
This is the cup I raise, pass to you.
Consider the cup.
Drink of it. All of you.
Born from the dream of this cup.
This is nourishment.
Each moment's beginning baptizes me.
Opening to myself I give birth.

•

You're a beat, Pa-Pa Lanto. You're a voice.

The universe, Keri, Keri,
goes around in rhythm.

Olatunji is a drum of passion, Pa-Pa Lanto.
The drum was forbidden, Pa-Pa Lanto.
We kept it in the back room, out of sight, ha-ha.
Discordant, Pa-Pa Lanto, too loud,
too much like your heartbeat, ha-ha.
Akiwowo, conductor of the train.
Akiwowo, conductor of the train.
Please take me home
To my father's house.
Akiwowo, conductor of the train.
Why are you afraid of your heartbeat?
Feel the puppy, Pa-Pa Lanto.
The pup puts her running shoe on your lap.
She wants to play. Akiwowo. A cappella.
Hold her head. She is listening. Look.
Se Eni A Fe L'Amo—Kere Kere
You Know The One You Love — Herald The News
The puppy knows. Feel the puppy.
Love the one you're with.
Aaron Neville sings this, too.
A kind of family joke, Pa-Pa Lanto.
Love the one that brought you down,
Ha-ha-ha. Ha-ha-ha.
Akiwowo, Akiwowo.

BOOK TWO

APPEAR AND INSPIRE

Book Two

APPEAR AND INSPIRE

"Yea, it is even he that shall keep thy soul."
—Psalm 121

A cat walks a morning roof line.
A choir sings the 23d Psalm. Each individual act

is a crime against the village.
Tears fill my eyes before such beauty.

In this house, on this morning, music
from my crossing, and Jesus:

If you bring forth what is in you,
what you have will save you.

In my evacuation dreams, I settle
inside a stone in the suburbs

against the desires of those
who want me to remain in the city.

I have everything I need.
There is some question about the pup.

Is she in or out?
She is at my side.

I am 40 days into year 7. The charmed life.
There is the question of the garden,

77 days under snow. What's going on
underneath the snow is wild.

•

WAITING FOR MORNING

My tongue finds a loose tooth. It turns
this tooth, tethered by the slightest of roots,
into a toy. Just as the tooth is about to break
free, the tongue, cruising the mouth,

discovers another tooth, also dislodged,
and then another. I am reporting a fragment
of last night's dream. I do not have a clue
to its meaning. Alarmed, the once playful

tongue, turns into a sentry inspecting
the mouth, and all of my teeth for loose moorings.
All of its suspicions are confirmed. All
of the teeth are unhinged. This is what

remains of the dream. Yesterday my friend
writes me a poem instead of a letter.
This is not unusual. He is my friend.
We run at the Y. Walk and run.

This playful puppy, turns vigilante.
I think about this as we run.
My friend talks about a man who falls,
a man who is a river and a city,

a man who shares his name with the destiny
of falling water. I want to talk about dreams,
a word held captive in the village. Falling,
I know, initiates the coming of the dream,

falling makes it possible to be a Moon Man.
I am an initiate. These are impersonal principles.
Poets embracing what's clever, not the dream itself.
Reining it in with a harness offers only

employment, yields only practicality.
All day I work on a list of things accomplished,
poems to keep the beast away. Praise
as obscenity and fear. Water runs off

our bodies. My friend has another word
for beginning, a word his townspeople call a crime.
We listen for what comes up, for what is given.
I add four lines to the résumé I put in the mail:

The puppy is on a leash and wants to run.
The mission of the tongue is to make the song.
Time spent baking bread is time spent near an oven.
All the teeth in the mouth break free.

•

MAKING APPLICATION

Memory is a kind
of accomplishment
a sort of renewal
even
an initiation, since the spaces it opens are new
places

Listen here, Paul Mariani, teacher of the American epic,

I might have started like this
in the old days, in the old life, from the other circle, far
from the four corners of things.

Unless there is a new mind

The blood of the fish is also the blood of Christ

I was a pretty small frog in a mighty big pool

The transition is dangerous. Blood might clot.

Thought this would be easy. Like listening to music—to Marsalis, on this path, through this garden—in this house,

and waiting

for song to work its way into—HA—

me.

Anyway,

I got started one morning in September
I remember feeling a long ways from my wife and pup.
I was back at work. It was like meditation.
And I would turn to it in between dreams.
And in between poems, I would put on music
and write, this path, this garden, this house.
And it becomes a way to music.

When I came back from Paterson, I got wind of you,
and after you replied, the poem changed,
it took off on its own, I took what the morning gave me,
I thought, here is a poem I can spend my life on,
On This Path...

Oh, I cruised, I tell you. I had Soma straight
from the Moon—the water man was dipping his cup
into the golden well—dreams spoke directly—
the house stood the storm of winter,
the poem changing all the time—a left-handed sailor—
guiding me—me thinking, finally a way
to put everything in.

And last week it changes again,
This time the critic—*his voice, one among many (unheard)*
moving under all. *The Mountain quivers.* I must do this thing,

I MUST BRING, SOMEHOW BRING, THIS CRITIC TO POWER
AND LET HIM BE HEARD, THAT THE 10,000 THINGS
IN THE 10,000 POEMS WILL SHOW THEMSELVES HERE, TOO.

This poem is no longer free.

Even this application to the epic

is being held to yesterday's work.

Beautiful thing. Take off your clothes.

✦

Lewis Hyde, gift-man in big books, says,
Berryman's talk is all booze.
I don't know anymore.
My new questions aren't so sure
of anyone who's certain.
I'm straight but not narrow
the bumper sticker reads.
I'm more inclined to think
we're all carrying the same stuff.
Everybody's carrying.
And so much of it systemic
in the culture. What pisses
me off about my friends in A.A.
besides all their talk about booze,
is they don't celebrate the Soma
in their own cups, and though
they are redeemed, as my friend says,
their talk keeps others from seeing
their own dangerous possibilities.
This is thrilling work.
Thrilling, and I don't think
any should be denied access.
There ought to be many ways,
many ways, *to turn my hand up*
and hold it open.

February 2-3, 1997

✦

Talk to him as a friend. Descend or die.

You crossed a leopard on the trail. That leopard's

waiting. I've heard that dream of the falling teeth,
but I've never heard it from the point

of view of the tongue. Such a puppy.
Sexual organ, first greeter of food, so quick

to hide from heat's extremes. Quick to run.
Anything other than descent is evasion.

Teeth are solid rocks, the foundation
the house was built on. Unmoored,

not one tooth, all teeth. Wholesale leaving.
I talked to a man whose entire jaw fell

from his face along with the teeth.
It's hard to trust the images we're given.

The symbolism of teeth will never be exhausted.
Teeth are deeply rooted. It's in your poem.

I wanted so hard to send in a greater dream.
I wanted to tell about the anointing. Or being

given the sacred denim. But I was bound
on the Wheel. I had to send the dream

I was given, not my greatest hits. The way
down is not through our strength but

our weakness. What's the line of Jesus
you didn't use: *If you don't use what's in you,*

you'll die. Those Gnostic gospels. It's hard
to trust the unconscious. One tradition says,

take in two dreams, one you want to talk about,
and one you don't. Talk about the one you fear most.

◆

Most of the people training dogs
are women. I've been one of three men
all winter. These women like the leash,
and they like dogs who obey. None of us
can hear ourselves talk to our dogs.
Last night this woman
starts urging her pup,
Get it up, Get it up.
What saved me the first time
I heard it is this,
I thought I heard it wrong.
Get it up, Get it up, she called,
calling for more. By then
I was one puppy on point,
I was one dog under command.
Get it up, Get it up, she said.
Like she's singing while dusting furniture.
And then there's me,
going back and forth
between this puppy
and a psychologist,
talking about dreams.
I was one drug store Indian
last night, no shaman
in this sweat lodge, my eyes grateful
for my pup, eyes never flinching,
anticipating the woman's command,
Get it up, Get it up.
Good puppy, Get it up.

•

to lead captivity captive
—Ephesians 4: 8

PASSING OUT PEDRO PÁRAMO

Everybody is already dead.
The past exists with the present
and the people of the past haunt

everybody. The difference
between dream and reality
is non-existent. Chronological time
is not a value. It's not important.
Internal time is opened up. Echoes

are the actions that repeat in the head.
Media Luna is the rancho.
Pedro Páramo, el cacique, el hacendado,
el patrón himself, is dead. *The patrón*

is dead. Are you listening?
You're already free.
Las cadenas que sentimos
existen adentro. Somos libres.

Juan Preciado is the *narrador*
but you won't know this until you
get to page 40, in English, that's 110
in the Spanish text. Echoes killed

everybody. *Pedro Páramo*
gets everything he wants but what
he wants. Susana San Juan.
Pedro Páramo tells the revolutionaries,

Join up with the side that's winning.
We're going to cut the spine off one book
and shuffle the pages. Someone will follow
the story with this text. It shouldn't make

any difference. Look at the ear
on the front cover, the eye on the back.
Susana, el pájaro de papel caía en maromas,
'Papalote', del Nahuatl, mariposa.

Look at the *calaveras* on the Spanish cover.
Ruidos. Voces. Rumores. Canciones lejanas,
That's my favorite line in the book.
Whose voices do you want to carry?

Pay attention to who's talking.

The voice you save must be your own.
Use time to get a foothold. Is this flashback,
retrospectiva? What grave are the characters

talking from? The grave of the cemetery?
Comala itself? or Hell? ¿Qué aburridas
are their lives? How much boredom
are you willing to put up with *en su propia vida?*

Explore silence. Move around in it.
Explore dreams. What divides living and dead?
They were leaping from memory to memory
desdibujando, *erasing* el presente.

Are you going to wait for an army of revolutionaries
to save your life? Or do you want to begin now?
Read the book. Write your way out of this grave place.
Give me your testament on freedom next Thursday.

Sea fuerte. Escribe desde su corazón.

✦

Giving up on rage doesn't mean giving up on anger.
My friend says, All art is made in anger. Anger,

of course, is a friend making great things happen.
Frustration's not anger. Inner work doesn't trade

anger for ease. A man shot full of holes
responds in many ways. An artist charged

with making a song calls on fuel from any well.
An artist responds to what he's been given.

Rave on through the writing of a vision.
The vision is the message given in dreams.

To speak free. To allow all to surface
and thrive. These are the politics

of coming clean. These are the politics

of the liberating voice. Everything false,
falls.—Now—dependent on no one.
Impersonal principles,

observable by any. Mystical practicality,
all change taking place within. What

disappears in the external world
disappears naturally—

And what about music?

I am charged to admire men.
A woman walks into the room,
hands me a volume of Blake
bound with plates the visionary
could never have imagined.
Her mother's valentine gift.
I open it to Blake's Milton,
a journey of self-discovery and renewal.
Milton returns from heaven to the mortal world
and unites with the imagination
through Blake.
In each moment I praise
what's admirable in men.
Milton unites with his feminine side,
an emanation named Ololon.
The division between the sexes is over.
Home from work I open Blake to Milton:
For in this Period the Poet's Work is Done...
Within a Moment
a Pulsation of the Artery.

I am fixing up a room for Judy.
She says the thin February sun
makes her feel better. She sends me
a letter and five poems, calls me
all of the things I want to be called.
Tapping into her adrenaline
I could tell her about Soma.
Judy's hip, funny. She writes about her body,
the altered state of dread being good for something.

She is a valkyrie. I want to be able
to call to her from the kitchen of this poem.
I want to go straight to code.
In these winter poems she writes,
I have to remind myself
that ever since
her sickness Mother's been numb
as a button.
I break into laughter during odd moments.
The last line of a short poem,
a fragment, holds me in a February chill.
I am this stranded miner's wife.
A son of an elevator operator,
cut loose from the grain.
Judy writes.
And then her pencil comes in
and wants to cut what's already spare,
and I lose my breath,
liking the prepositional phrase
that includes, and centers her,
not slung low around the kitchen sink,
but in the stars themselves,
The long handle
curving away (from her) hiding animals.
Without consulting Blake
she frames her own room
in the Yakima sky,
tossing in pages of epigrams.
I build the room around Judy's violin,
a dirty animal. I'll let my fingers drum ebony.

•

PUTTING MY BELT BUCKLE BACK ON MY BELT, I SAY
TO THE CRAFTSMAN, 'IF I HAD THESE JEWELS INSIDE ME NOW
I MIGHT NOT NEED THE ADORNMENT ON THE OUTSIDE':
THIS IS THE LESSON IN THE JEWELRY

> *Afterwards when the light of the flaming sun went under*
> *they went away each one to sleep in his home where for each one*
> *the far-renowned strong-handed Hephaisto had built a house*
> *by means of his craftsmanship and cunning.*

The Iliad of Homer

My friend Lovins puts Lockup in my hands.
Lockup, a belt buckle, hammered
into a warrior's shield by Lovins
eight years ago. Gift from Hephaisto.
Made for a poem binding me to my life.
Lovins puts it in my hands,
refurbished, retooled. A belt buckle

for a man cut loose, unmoored,
binding himself to vision alone,
and the ruler of the imagination.
See Visions, Dream Dreams, & Speak Parables—
against all claims of the world. Poetry
itself, dead except for the business of it,
owned & operated by the universities, &

mega-booksellers with bar-codes
for gates where paint brushes might be.
Distributors taking 60% of the book
they won't market unless it can make payment
on their insurance. Poetry, chained to small
presses chained to small themes of anger and justice—
the political poem of despair and boredom. Armed

with a belt buckle and the courage of no agenda,
a man embarks. He doesn't know where he's going
but he will die if he stays; he goes willingly,
in joy, not happiness. Happiness. A word
that must remain behind in the village.
This is the story of our time. The man
must leave behind his family and go.

He wears a belt buckle and a vest and no agenda.
On his vest is a pin. Lovins calls it a mountain.
The man knows the mind has mountains, too.
He calls the mountain, a wolf's tooth set in silver,
a weapon. He crossed a leopard on the trail.
The man questions himself, even when
he knows, *Must I also leave my friends?*

The desert floor he seeks is his own.

The descent is only into himself. The man wears
a medicine box forged by Lovins. For years the man
tried to be grateful. He thought of Achilleus' shield
every time he put it over his heart. Now he was making
the heart's journey. Images that adorn the box:
a mountain, a spot of gold, Song lines. Inside

the box: a power rod, a broken circle, a button
from his wife's sewing box, toe bone from a coyote
from the Reservation at Pine Ridge, 3 coins
for throwing the I Ching (made for this box by Lovins),
a pebble from a hike into Goat Rocks Wilderness, and
a piece of lead type, capital letter I, first person pronoun,
the letter earned for the one who goes

inside to make a way. The charmed man.
Lockup. This is all there is to freedom.
The relationship that is changed
is the relationship to oneself. Perhaps
this is why others think they've been abandoned.
The man gives life to himself
after all these years of self-denial and hate,

after giving what he had to others they came,
perhaps, unknowingly, to expect it from him.
(Perhaps his giving denied them their own mountains.)
Conversion takes place near here.
People freeze, lock-up, caramelize their crystal, stay home.
The village says, He quit drinking. He gave up cigarettes.
Neither is this about women, or giving up wild ways.

For once, at last, this is about being wild.
The real wilderness. *How to find the way in?*
Most who quit anything quit here.
The man wears many vests. Each of the vests hand-made
by his wife. Each of the vests displaying colors,
textures the man has never seen in himself. Each vest
sacred, each vest displaying a different pin from Lovins,

his jeweler, his Hephaisto, his sHADOWmARKED friend.
Lovins has been sHADoWmARKED. He is a fire god.
Art cannot contain his vision. He's a teacher, a visionary,

but the schools, public and private, are village schools.
The schools are being taught by Congress
and the President of the United States of America.
The curriculum director, a woman on the outside,

is all rubbed up by the Rotary Club. On his green
Pendleton vest, so rich and deep and quiet it makes
him cry putting it on, (his mask won't hold), he wears
a cluster of boulders hammered from soft metal.
He weeps because he has moved into these stones.
He shelters here, in these rocks, on this most
unsuspecting of vests. *I have been given so much*

from others. The man who leaves lives outside
of time. Adorning his Silver Anniversary Vest
is a lighthouse. The lantern is a pomegranate seed.
Each vest, every lapel, tracks the man's leaving.
Each contains a story. The man is given these gifts
by those who love him, partly for his determination
to go, and partly for his leaving. Lovins, his wife,

a couple of friends who write him poems.
The village condemns each individual act,
requiring one more shield. Lovins' fingers covered
this shield for his 50th year, buffalo hide stretched thinner
than onion skin over a frame of balsa wood. It hangs
on a wall in a house built for poems. For the solitary,
there will be few friends, and many guides. This shield

is a witness made by the man in the Moon.
Believing in the guides gives a man some sleepless nights.
The shield carries images from his battles, his shadowmARK,
these words: *cost of the stars, Crazy Horse, thick ears,*
besides passion everything is grass, and some comics.
The man buckles up. The way in is through the weaker side,
a blind alley requiring endless chants of love.

for Marty Lovins

61, 66, 73

•

Waking to the sounds in desdibujando,
I begin a chant taking me inside the visions—
las visiones de los jovenes—
Desdibujando, desdibujando.
Des dibujo, des dibujo. The drawing.
Des the drawing. Erase the drawing.
Dis in the language of the street young.
To dis someone. *To off them. Disappear them.*
Erase. Eraser. I can see the eraser. Erasure.
Desdibujándolo. Desdibujándole.
Their visions on paper that consumed me last night.
These visions are different. Not *....des dibujos...*
Disappearing the present.
Leaping from memory to memory.
The last great lines in Rulfo's little book,
his gigantic dream, the line arrives with Blake.

See visions,
dream dreams,
speak parables.
This is daily life.
This is what to expect.
What to prepare for.
This is an agenda.
This is a house
with many rooms.

Blake and Rulfo in the same room.

Build that.

In this house.

Imagine that.

✦

ALL OF THE NAMES NOT RECORDED HERE ARE CARVED INTO THE STONES AT MACCHU PICCHU. MACCHU PICCHU ITSELF HAS BEEN MOVED TO MANY PLACES AND RENAMED. SOMOS MUCHOS. EVERYONE IS STILL WITH US.

DREAM DREAMS, SEE VISIONS, SPEAK PARABLES.
LAURA ESQUIVEL JOINS JUAN RULFO AND WILLIAM BLAKE
ON THE TRAIL. PABLO NERUDA ASKS ALL SCHOOL BOARDS
IN AMERICA TO TAKE HIS BOOKS OFF THE SHELVES
IN THE NAME OF DREAMERS.
SIDDHARTHA EVA VALDIVIA NAMES HERSELF,
AND THIS POEM CELEBRATES HER NAMING. TOM HASSLINGER JOINS US,
AND ADALBERTO LOPEZ. THE LANDSCAPE IS CHANGING.
THIS PATH, THIS GARDEN, THIS HOUSE.
THIS IS THE HOUSE OF DREAMERS. ALL DREAMERS
WHO ACTUALLY DREAM DREAMS AND SEE VISIONS ARE MOVING IN.
BEGIN WITH ALMA VARELA AND HER SISTER YOSHIMI VARELA,
VERDADERAS ABRECAMINOS ALONG WITH THEIR SISTER CECILIA WHO LED
THEM HERE. OPEN YOUR THICK EARS. THE PATHWAY IS HERE.

Alma's vision begins, Como Agua Para Chocolate—
towards liberation and eternity.

I put the clothes in the dryer and they almost burned
but they came out like just ironed. La comida es lo primero,

si es que hay algo que se sabe hacer, es cocinar.
I think we wouldn't be Mexicans if we didn't cook. When

you cook, you feel the power of knowing. The power
that can never be known unless you cook. Como yo,

cuando recuerdo el "chicharrón con Nopales en Chile Verde"
que hacíamos en la casa, que olor, un olor que entra

por la nariz, y entra al organismo. Ésto es vida.
Salsa Verde. Una palabra muy amplia. I can't forget

how to cook, that's something you bring from heaven
and you take it back to heaven. You just got to live

the way you cook. Tita was furious in the kitchen.
The questions she didn't have in the kitchen,

she had in the world. All of this gave her hunger,
hunger in the heart, hunger of love, hunger in freedom,

hunger in herself. But Pedro, he was the one,
just like a piece of Mondango, with that creamy flavor.
That's what Pedro was. Mondango. Nothing is ever perfect
in this world of order and sounds. I didn't know

what a Mexican meal meant, till I didn't make it anymore,
till I didn't have my mother make it for me. I didn't know

what to be a Mexican is, till I became a gabacha,
then I found out who I really like to be. I want

to keep being Mexican because it's good, because
Como Agua Para Chocolate wouldn't exist

if there weren't Mexican women with imagination
to show life to the world. Because I see the difference

in my personalities. Our fosforos have to be discovered,
and no way can you fear, no time to wait for someone

else to come light our matches. y así como un poeta juega
con las palabras. I realize I need care from myself.

I come from a place even when I don't live there.
I can be reunited with myself. La vida que todos

deseamos imaginar y escuchar. Tita and Pedro
died of love because their truth made them free—

of course earthly life is supposed to be fun too.
They just went to a more free place.

•

The other side of passion and wonder, Yoshimi,
Alma's sister, writes, They say she was born crying.
Why, I ask myself? I don't have my mother with me;
instead I have my sister. But no one will be like my

mother. I know I need her warm hands, her warm arms,
her words, her company. I can feel she lives in me,

and that was something Tita never figured out. It would
be hard not to be able to develop your own culture.

Maldita decencia! Sometimes we don't do what our hearts
tell us to do. Sometimes we just take directions. During
these times I've been away from my parents I see
things from another point of view. El que nadie se coma

el último chili de una charola, generalmente sucede
cuando la gente no quiere demostrar su gula
y aunque les encantaría devorarlo, nadie se atreve.
It's true, isn't it? It's hard to have the nerve to take

the last chile. They know it's delicious. They know
the taste is great, but they don't want to look like a
glutton. Who cares about what you do? If you don't
do it because of them, will it help you in some way?

Will they give you the power you could have had
from that chili? ¿Qué importa la sociedad? ¿Qué importa
si ellos hablan de ti o no? I'll have my illusion, my dream.
My life the way I want to live it. I want to be in that

Magical Realism. Writing this, my heart
feels great joy. There is something inside my body
that gives me happiness. Cuando respiro, respiro
con una ilusion, con alegría, con libertad,

con ánimo de hacer, lo que yo quiero,
lo que yo deseo. ¡Que vida! A dream is life.
A dream keeps us alive. It makes us fight,
live without air, e inclusive ir al más alla,

a lugares nunca antes vistos. These two,
the special sisters. The fifty-plus who crossed
the waters of Wilkamayu, also know
El Río Bravo. They all have visions, they all

bring the dreams. We will no longer write
essays. Only visions and dreams. Daily life.
Siddhartha Eva Valdivia who named herself
because she didn't have a name, remembers

an uncle who made her read a book
before going out to play. I told him it wasn't fair.
He told me unfair would be keeping me away
from the knowledge that is available

to better know life. He said, You see this book?
And that one? And that other one? And all of them?
All these are your future, the beginning,
the wisdom, your opportunity to succeed—

and I read you a book so you won't be stubborn
like your mother, and know about life,
and not be what people say. These are visions
the curriculum director tried to keep the visionaries

from having. Adalberto López writes of semillas,
seed thoughts. When you taste Mexican food
like tortas de navidad o Tortas de Camarones
con Remeritos, you remember the Aztecas,

when they got to the great Tenochtitlán
and saw an eagle standing on a Nopal devorando
una serpiente. Or when you taste los frijoles de hornilla,
you can imagine when Cuauhtemoc was being burned.

Tom Hasslinger stays clean reading with the Mexicanos,
the lone gabacho. Love, like the bullet that's chasing me,
knows no rules, Tom writes. I can break away
and live life as an individual, not polluting my mind

or body, for myself, for life, for true living.
José Lozano reads his book with his mother
and writes of family secrets, his title adding,
And Don't Forget This Nice Family. José dreams

literature dreaming him: Literature looks like
a Mexican way, like when I was in the barrancas
in my little ranchito I was very poor. Sometimes
I didn't have no food to eat, for I can eat all this,

literature acts as a mirror, when I go to a mirror
I remember that literature is my life, I am

peinándome my hair. I love to work on farms.
I used to plant a lot of different plants

for every one can eat these poems in the book.
The formality of these lines baffles me.
I am lifting visions at random.
Each dreamer loaded with gold—hard rock

miners—alchemists would plant pots from Safeway
in their cookware reading these parables.
These are daily visions. Among visionaries
and dreamers, is one dream greater than

another? Jesús Soto is not into literature.
But this book is different from any other book,
it has stuff of how it really is in our Mexican culture,
because we really like to joke a lot. What I carry

from this novel is the passion of life
by just being yourself. Soto is himself
a parable, a dream, and a great visionary.
Miriam Díaz titles her vision, No longer Alone,

Raising my eyes to see the Virgin Mary
I can remember so many things, but
really what I can't remember is when
I started crying for the truth.

I do not distinguish among dreamers.
I do not need to ask where I leave off
and where the other visionaries begin.
Las fronteras en el mundo de los sueños no existen.

•

PUPPY SPIRIT

BREAK CHAINS
MAKE THE WAY
SEA ABRECAMINOS
ONLY CARRY WHAT WE NEED
STAY TOGETHER

DREAM DREAMS
ROMPER CADENAS
SEE VISIONS
SPEAK PARABLES
LOOK FOR OURSELVES
LEARN THE FLOWERS
TRAVEL LIGHT

✦

SPEAK IN PARABLES

What do you think I'm doing, William Blake.
For the love of Jesus, I wake hours before
Karen or the puppy, chanting,
See visions, dream dreams, speak in parables.
I get up, inside the poem already,
wrapped tight in your wild music.

Yesterday is up in smoke.
Karen drives to Seattle so I can build the time.
I move the chocolate visions into the house.
Karen, still working on family drama,
carries photos to a mountain retreat
with five women mapping themselves,

(Karen carried the dreams inside),
five who brought her forward.
Karen saying to me, Jim,
You don't have to justify the dream.
Karen says the whistling in the engine
is only air going through the ski rack.

We're in the year 30-49 right now.
Paula enters the room this fast.
The divine is always in reverse.
The figure 8 is infinity.
This is the dream I was given.
This doubling exists in any myth.

I'm not alone in here. Karen had her dreams first.
I can hear Aaron Neville.

Danger and joy are parts of the same moment.
A woman makes a drawing from another woman's poems.
Visions cross.
The woman is at the center of her dream.

A father promises his daughter a horse.
She waits. She is a good daughter.
He is a man of God. Everyone loves him.
She waits for years. She waits for that moment
when she will no longer be a child.
This is the horse he cannot remember.

Of course, he says, of course.
This is his vodka dream.
Karen drives the car carrying the horse
the woman's been dreaming for forty years.
It's hers. It's running wild. The horse
carries her into her life. Her horse is

dreaming her. The notebook is a wild horse
going back and forth between two worlds.
We carry the vision knowing we're knocking
on the door of the world. Close the door to survive.
Put the story of your life into this pony.
Become a poet to retrieve the story.

Being able to respond. I walk out of a restaurant.
The wall of a woman's book store painted
with the words, Response Able. Aunt Marjorie
saved a rocking chair for Karen in Indiana.
She had to go back to get it. Being able to dream.
Seeing visions. Speaking in parables. I wake

this morning from a road dream.
I am a roadie. A man carrying the guitars
of women. The women are a band of musicians.
This is a working dream. We are on the road.
They have to stop and pee. It is a slow go.
I tap a tambourine at my side.

THE JELLY OF THANKSGIVING

Some people call this jelly,
the Jelly Of The Way It Is.
This is not the jelly our mothers
taught us to make, and neither

is it the jelly we set out to make ourselves.
Still, it's a good jelly,
and it's made the same way.
The old recipes, after all, go way,

way back. Our mothers
were only passing them on.
It's from a wine grape. But the giddiness
comes from a bubble inside yourself.

BOOK THREE

The William Stafford Rooms

Music is soma and so are you, Mr. Stafford.

Book Three

◆

SOMA IN THE KITCHEN

◆

You can build me a cabin in Montana,
Karen says, but you'll have to bury me
in this house. I'm never leaving this house.

◆

VALENTINE'S POEM, FOR KAREN

In the kitchen, this morning
with Karen, the day before Valentine's,
Karen tells me her dream:

I'm climbing a ladder of 2 x 4's.
I'm in the basement,
climbing to an upper room,

—You're doing such good work,
I interrupt—But wait,
I don't make it, Karen says,

reclaiming her dream—
This handmade ladder
comes completely apart,

—me thinking, Don't fall, don't fall—
I don't make it, I'm falling.
The 2 x 4's have broken free.

I almost steal the dream.
Karen tells it, *I don't make it.* Falling,
we're really ascending in love.

⬩

You are the original idea,
come to me in a Spokane hotel room,
in my daily kitchen.
You are the dream of the oatmeal cookie.

⬩

SOMA IN THE KITCHEN

Sitting here with you, William Stafford,
taking Soma in the kitchen, makes this room

yours. Nothing calculated happens here,
no pretenders. The little adventures

arriving in the cup always arrive as miracles
come from the moon. *The chosen must*

survive as they are made. I still marvel
at how you served up pure Soma, left all,

almost all, biography behind. Your crossing
to the dream side still bewilders the politics

of the poem. Fear and shame keep even
the best poets locked out of their lives. Once

the clever mask comes down, the Soma runs.
Is there bread for this hunger? What we do

in this early morning kitchen is listen. Sometimes
my wife walks in unannounced, surprising me,

surprised to find me blasted, blitzed by the moon.
There are rooms in a house, this one is yours.

✦

LACY DREAMWALKER

The pup is already orphaned.
She belongs to life.

✦

SOLITARY SKIER

for my daughter, Krista

At the trail markers,
Midway — Hourglass

Out of the wind I relish
(we relish)—
Wind, Krista, speed, the swirl of it all:

Beautiful thing!

Where we skied just four days ago,

I hear your voice

responding to your sensitive ear

You got a poet's ear, Krista,
wondering

where your mother
fits into the I of my voice

We are voices We are birds of fire We sing with our life

SPEAK PLAIN SO I DON'T HAVE TO READ
BETWEEN THE LINES!

Your Mother and I love each other very much.
We're fated. You don't have to worry about us.

We're trying to go inside the I, the I each of us
brings to this long marriage—*Beautiful thing!*

The marriage of two people
doesn't really work
isn't magic
until two people
can experience marriage
with the self.

Mystical union!

It makes no sense unless
it can be observed by all.
Look, you live by yourself

Because you can live with yourself
doesn't guarantee you can live with others,
but you can't live with others
until you can live with yourself.

I'm alone on this mountain

a solitary skier   in the wind

This can be seen—but there are others on the mountain too!

There are mountains in the mind

We're all looking for a way down the mountain

The way down is the way inside

That's the trick of courage,

Krista, skiing Roller Coaster, you asked me for a challenge

Finding a way inside

is the challenge   *Beautiful thing!*

Guilt & Shame bar the door

Culture police dressed to dance and teach

Break through them

You have the passion!

You have the best chance of any

because you don't close the door.

I'm under trees now

not quite out of snow. Wind
curls the snow around the fir
where I sit writing

In a temple of trees

The ink dissolving into snow flakes
settling on the page

Beautiful thing!

Opening up trails in the inner world back country

Everyone equal, each a beginner, no right, no wrong

Nobody ahead nobody behind a solitary skier

sees himself in a temple of trees

loses himself in a temple of trees

sings to himself in a temple of trees

he is a voice

to his daughter

with the sensitive ears

A solitary dancer A teacher closer to her students than her own profession

The bird is the thing I couldn't see on my own

Those who imagine themselves over the edge

will find a way

The way up is the way down

The way down is the way inside

•

RED RIBBON

Krista, your new place seems complete.
Photos, music, candles,
Calico, the 15-year-old cat you grew up with.
These lines praise you, red ribbons.
Your place is a way station, a place to settle
when there's nothing more to give.
Krista, you're the package, each day a door to yourself.
You are the entry into the room,
the voice on the phone sayiing, Hello.
You have chosen the way of wild giving,
burning passion,
a seeker of justice, lover of all children.
You believe all children come from love.
Living your love is your chosen road.
You carry the voice of your father,
your grandmother, and your great grandmother, Myra.
70 years of great giving.
It's yours. An inheritance.
Krista,
you have been given apprenticeship.
It is the long way of the pickpocket.
It is given to those who have chosen missions.
You have seen me shield my eyes before your fire.
Stand before this great adventure.

Once, on a family picnic, a spider
crossed the blanket where your cousin Megan lay playing.
Three days later the spiders attacked you.

While the spiders came from all sides
I carried you while they held you in terror.
Then I ate them one at a time until they could no longer multiply,
until you could see for yourself, until you, too,
could gain courage to face the fear, and you did,
and we finished them in a day, popping them
into our mouths like candy.

You have chosen to be fire.
What I turn away from
I haven't learned to love in myself.
Energy is sacred
You are only love.

✦

HEAR THIS.

STRANGE COMPANIONSHIP

Five miles from the mountain
the sun shines. The mystery is not less
because it has been given language.
I watch my son, effortless, descending

a mountain of pitch and terror,
a descent made possible by music.
The dream world makes day life rich, too.
Day light feeds the dream. The mystery

of skis tuned by music. My observations
of a son who knows how to fall
brings me only joy.
Why am I in tears? Mystery includes

the known as well as the unknown.
The dream says a man must put aside
personal considerations. The skis
have their own gravity. The body

gives itself up to eternity and chance.
I have myself on this mountain,

strange companionship. Wind swirls;
I disappear, snowing and blowing.

✦

CUTTING VEGETABLES

Evening is morning, too.
Sliced onions under a sharp knife

on the cutting board makes a kind
of percussion. Goethe is crying,

Two souls are housed within my head.
I do not go against myself. I slice

four cloves of garlic so thin
it browns on contact in olive oil.

Two pizzas, each with its own secret.
I love the pleasure of brushing the dough

in oil before painting it with sauce.
The dream serves up the evening meal.

For twenty years I thought it was me
doing all this cooking. The stone

in this oven is not for bread alone.
Karen will be home in a few minutes,

or she might not be. Ten minutes
in the oven is all it takes to meet

all the figures of the epics.
If I can see the great story in my life

I can write it. Going into the oven
isn't imagination, it's daily life.

✦

DINING WITH KAREN

Karen eats one piece of pizza
before running off to ring the bells.
Ring the bells, I say, hoping the music
running from me can be of some use,

knowing how far Karen can throw
sound with her strong hands around
the brass bells. Sounds far sweeter
than the pineapple I tuck into mozzarella

with my fingers. Each has its own
memory. It is my responsibility to bring
all I have to all that comes to me. This is not
a trick and requires training beyond

sitting here, tonight. I'm not just listening
to music, Mama man, I'm making music.
The meaning of blood can be tracked
directly from Christ to the union

of opposites. Here, one is not too far
from drunkenness or the Red Sea.
Some of this Karen knows;
some of it she's not interested in.

It is a sin to want to remain unconscious.
The kitchen knows my ashes and my fire.
Six minutes with Karen is more than I ask for.
I report what comes from the oven.

✦

EARLY MORNING DREAMS

✦

LISTENING TO BOB MARLEY'S FREEDOM SONGS

✦

READING THE MAIL

✦

LETTERS FROM THE FOUR CORNERS

Dear Ones, is how Mary's letters arrive
from Indiana. Her son's second daughter,
an early arrival, gives life as she fills her lungs,
tiny thimbles, with air. Grandmother and nurse,
midwife to Karen's story, family archivist,
Mary's news walks us around points of diamonds.
David and Ian are traveling to North Carolina
to see their mom in school. She cuts the grandson's
hair, but leaves the pony tail braid tucked
into the back of his shirt. Her daughter, Beth,
now has a rabbit, two goats, and a black lab, Ali;
Mary hopes the animals will hold them in Indiana,
even as they feel their calling in Salvador.
Arvin, her husband, continues with his Hebrew.

Gayle sends February: The Hard Noise of Winter,
for the Poetry Pole. She is telling the world
everything it needs to know. She has a place to wail.
The Pole rejects nothing. She tells me about salmon
in huckleberry sauce, snow ghosts and ice crystals.
She takes care of her father. She knows he
is her way home. She's been on a train.
She writes from the desert in Eastern Washington.
She says this: But now I am back.
She tells me about my dreams
and her daughters moving step by step.
The long letter she wrote has disappeared,
into the new technology;
daughters, sleeping dogs and husbands.

From Brooding Heron Press & Bindery
on Bookmonger Road at Waldron Island
in the San Juans, Sam Green sends me a note
along with Judy's poems bound on boards.

Local politics has gotten nasty. They have been
giving testimony to County Commissioners.
He reports lies, misleading information, half-truths.
No fun, he says, ugly, ugly. He says, *This is likely*
to be a permanent situation now as the world
fills up and places like this come under siege.
We're struggling to preserve a real community,
the way Berry defines it. The assholes on the other
side could not care less. We continue to print, to bind,
to write, and to look for wholeness where we can.

Because the theme was Valentine's Day, Zev says.
Zev's in the Bronx. *I wanted to come on as a wit*
more than visionary poet. Realized that's been
my thing with poetry for past decade, and what's wrong
with that? Zev's in New Jersey. *I like to write.*
The main thing now is authentic, ironic,
living the life with an intimate distance that draws
a mild grin, belly laugh. I want to keep tools sharp
and honest so I'll be ready to mine the stuff...
the idea is to be ready. I ask Zev about writing
and prayer. *I used to think poetry and journal*
writing was a form of prayer, but decided
it was too high on the mountains, and prevented
pleasure, insights, laughter. Thanks for asking.

—Hola, ¿Como estás? m'hija escribe de Morelia,
donde ella estas estudiando.
—Yo estoy bien. Espero que tu tambien
¡Saque dos 10's en mis examenes! ¡Estoy emocionado!
Mis clases estan bien pero hoy aprendi a conjugar en un tiempo
que esta muy dificil. Es el subjunctivo. !Es muy dificil para mi!
Mi maestra le dijo a mi clase que a nadie le gusta enseñarlo
y a nadie le gusta aprenderlo. ¡Me dio gusto oir esto! El viernes
Hope, Sherie y yo vamos al bar ver
el baile de los viejos. Estoy emocionada. Esta
es su ultima presentaión. Bueno. Tengo sueño porque
no me gusta escribir nada más en español. Leah.

•

THIS PATH, THIS GARDEN, THIS HOUSE

•

KAREN ASKS

And I am answering, and I'm nothing
if not grateful. These cookies.

Are you making those cookies for a reason?
Or are you making them to be making them?

Is it too much trouble to answer me?
I am mixing in toffee bits. I don't want her to see.

But it isn't that. It's her question, and her follow-up.
She's asking about my heart. This is the dream

of the oatmeal cookie. I will hide nothing.
I don't really know. I'm trying to bake

the ultimate cookie. I don't want to become bread.
I want to be this cookie. I don't know yet

if I'm making them for anybody. *I was thinking*
about your question. Maybe I would make a plate

for the secretaries. Maybe put a plate for teachers.
I could take a cookie up to the art room

for Sue and Judy, and Marty and Barry.
I got lost for a second, thinking how those names

looked just like that. You could take a plate
to work. It isn't that I wasn't listening, Karen,

it's your question. Such a question.
So many answers. And then there's you.

I'm making this cookie for you. But first,
first, it's for me. It's a dangerous cookie.

•

Released from the dream,
I record the details on the memo pad.
Last night I'm in camp
in the Rockies for two weeks. Women and men.
And young people. Not everyone's in tents
but we put tents up preparing to go out.
My notebook fills with memos.
There's a shopping mall
that catches the eye of some, this mall
serves as a motivator for me
to hit the trail. Two men warn me
that we can't go out. Rumors of an Australian
Wolf Dog, a bitch separated from her pups
blocks the trail ahead.

Today is a full moon. Lacy's beside our bed.
She waits for me as I track the dream. She
stretches before me, a dream herself, offering
a front leg, her head on my foot. I lightly work
the tendons before moving to her belly.
She stays until I pat her, OK,
a sign to wake Karen. She finds Karen
going under her arms, up into her face,
licking all the while. She licks Karen,
licks herself and licks Karen again.

Blake asked for eternity, and he got it.
I want to know my own averted face in the mirror.
The puppy scratching at the door.
This is a vision of the shattered cathedral.
Childish games played with zeal. Committed,
absolutely to the urge coming from within,
to the link between two levels of experience.

I'm standing in the garden room
holding a chain saw when Karen appears
with a drawing of her dream. The ladder
from the cellar, leads towards the light.
She draws in charcoal. The greatest dream
in the world is a woman wrestling with God.

Fallen limbs from the November storm
served to protect the roses. Karen smiles.
This is cleanup with a chainsaw.
Jacob and the ladder speaks to us outside of time,
pitched, as it is, in stony soil and given to the poor.
That which dreams through us connects us.
Not a flower is lost in the wreckage.
I ask to see the drawing again.
The biographer will explain away the visions
to help the reader understand. The spirits Blake
observed were real enough, they were the angels
of his childhood reading. Inspired introspection.
I ask Karen to listen to the music.
I prune a frozen branch from the Japanese Maple,
paint it in tar. It is one story for a house
to stand after a storm. I never expected
these flowers in the garden.

✦

Stafford's lines read like Blake's.
You can lie at a banquet, but you have to be
honest in the kitchen. There would be no
books without Karen. Catherine Blake
helps turn her husband into a parable.
And none can tell how from so small a center comes
such sweets,
I had to destroy the cornerstone I had built.
A flavor like wild honey begins
when you cross the river. Karen gives pieces
of herself to each of us at great cost. Catherine said,
You know dear, the first time you saw God
you were four years old—it set you to screaming.
Blake holds the sun in his right hand
as he pushes open the door to himself in Jerusalem.
The mail comes in hard on men and marriage.
There are rooms in a life, apart from others,
rich with whatever happens. Milton goes in
through Blake's foot, sees further, but doesn't know
who it is. Writing lines from Stafford's poems
gives such pleasure, but I break his lines in other ways.
Reach me my things, Blake calls to Catherine

in a vision. Beloved. *The money is going, Mr. Blake.*
Helpmate. I am so afraid of men. Oh, damn the money.
It becomes impossible to track the voices.
But you can follow the story.
Stafford rocks from a limb in a high oak.
A quality of attention has been given you.
Karen says, *I don't get a thing from working*
with the poems, but I enjoy being with you.
Catherine is our witness: He is always in Paradise.
Every little act, Word, work & wish, all remaining still.

•

Baby coyotes sit on chairs next to wolves.
The coyotes are playing with the wolves
who appear to be blind. The wolves have tape
over their eyes. The mischievous coyotes
sneak around the wolves's heads to get the tape.
The coyotes work hard to keep from being seen.
They don't want to be discovered as coyotes.
They want to know more about the blindness of wolves.

•

María needs a new kidney
but won't get it until her donor finishes school.
He keeps dropping this class he needs to pass.
María makes a collage from her Pedro Páramo vision.
She says, We are all dead. We live in our memory.
We have hallucinations we can't control.
When her mother comes back from Mexico
she locks herself in her bedroom for two weeks.
Her father has died. María lifts Rulfo from Comala
and puts his voice on the wall:
We may doze a little, sometimes,
but we never stop thinking. *¿Porqué?*
she asks, *¿porque?* I was making tortillas
and my hermano Pollo came and asked if I could help
him in his school work. So I did.
A-B-C-D-E-
Oh, that sweet memory.
—*¡Yara se te van a quemar las tortillas!*

My mom called me from her room. But it was
like if something was taking me away.
Pollo keeps on going, E-F-G-H-I-J—
Juan Preciado honors his mom's last wish.
The Media Luna—Pedro Páramo's world.
Mr. Bodeen, some people did not listen
to the dream. Now I hope
you can listen to my dream.
Money was everything to him—*qué pendejo.*
We are not dead, we are just hungry.

Yoshimi thinks these things happen too,
we just don't say them, we try not to see them.
Maybe they're normal to us. Everybody
asks me why. They say, I don't get it.
I got to the point: There is a big truth.
Cindy García, bilingual, bicultural,
travels to Jalisco while we read,
carries her book like she's on a school field trip,
no big deal, and hands me her vision
the day she returns. She says nothing to the class.
Las tumbas de Comala. Everyone's grave is different.
Cada uno de nosotros tenemos una tumba.
A secret that's buried.
Hay otros que mueren en su propia tumba.
Even after death the search continues.
Buscando algo que nunca hallaran.
Alma says Susana is as tall as Heaven.

✦

This is the meaning of blood.
The blood of the individual has been mapped
to Christ at the center by old man Edinger.
The shades of the dead in Hades could be restored
by giving a man a cup of blood to drink. He charts
a four-square vision. Sacrifice. From the top,
on one side is the priest, on the other is the victim.
To the left is the grape.
I have counted the number of leaves necessary
to produce sugar in one cluster.
The dream is also a suitable church,

The blood of the lamb runs in a mirror vision.
Guilt and vengeance continue the descent
tracking the blood, to what? Rivers? Trails?
All ways to Christ, and around Christ.
On one side, the wine press.
We've been on the wine press too long.
Here, with the grape, violence and inspiration.
Dismemberment and ecstasy are side by side.
The chalice serves up nourishment of milk and water.
The Solution is the containment of opposites at the bottom.
On the other side, underneath the lamb,
runs the lion and the dragon. One descends through wrath.
The dragon is tracked to fire. It is as important
to be slain by the dragon as it is to slay him.
Here is the red rose, eros, and light.
And bloody sweat. Out here, on the edge, is the word,
testing ordeals, and the Red Sea. Ha. Here
is the philosopher's stone. This is the meaning of blood.
This is the dream of opposites.
Heart, soul, and desire connect directly to Christ
from this side, mirroring nourishment and wine.

✦

LACY KNOWS

When I leave
to go inside
this poem

She's no longer
under command
And she goes

✦

The trombone, the dog working on a bone.

✦

The leash.

◆

REVOLUTIONARY LINES FOR MY SON ON HIS 26TH BIRTHDAY

The characters are real.
I do not make them up. Coyotes and wolves

are going at it, playing their hearts out.
There's a revolution going on inside me.

Skiing with you, how could I be
anything but a revolutionary? Right now,

in a sin against nature, the wolves are blind.
The coyotes are pups pulling at their patches,

teasing as much as fighting. Foxlike, tricksters,
the coyotes confuse the wolves, keep them

off-balance. I'm bound to this dream.
The coyotes and the wolves—both

of them running wild in me,
and I'm bound to follow. Dreams

hit us in our blind spots.
Oedipus with his eyes out.

Censored desire. How did the wolf go blind?
Who would blindfold wolves? The coyotes

take people across the river. The cork
is out of my bottle. All energies released

into the conscious world. I'm on a mountain
swirling into an hourglass. I'm playing

in the snow, a puppy of a father, singing
praises to my son descending the mountain.

Happy Birthday. Love, Dad

✦

THE INSISTENCE OF LACY

I am more than your Soma.
Make eye contact, Big Dog.

✦

—Titles for Kevin

READING YOUR LETTER DURING A CURRICULUM MEETING

"THEY WILL TELL A STORY IN FOUR COMPLETE SENTENCES"

WHEN I LOST IT

ONE OTHER THING ON MY SON'S BIRTHDAY

HOW YOUR "LETTERS OF RECOMMENDATION" GOT ME IN TROUBLE

HOW YOUR "LETTERS OF RECOMMENDATION" SAVED ME

LETTER TO KEVIN FROM THE KITCHEN AFTER THE CURRICULUM MEETING

CHOOSING MY FAVORITE LETTER

for Kevin

It's my son's birthday. He's 26.
On this night, on that day,
I was closer to Poor Tom on the heath
than I was to my wife and son. I see better, tonight,
and belong, like the puppy belongs,
to what life brings.
I open the barbecue for the first time.
There's snow on the ground.
Shannon, Tim's bride, made him a bracelet.
Karen and I buy the young lovers
a hotel room and two ski tickets in Oregon.
Honeymoon. Your wife's studying Spanish?
Give her this: *Luna de miel.*

It's poetry night in the Kiva.
Grimes is covering it. He's got posters
of Springsteen and Dylan all over school.
The basketball team shoots for the playoff
and our big gun is out with a bad ankle.
Honeymoons aren't only for newlyweds.
I had one today, too. A short one. With your letter.
I try to stay quiet, to say to myself,
Whoever I judge, I will become.
I came home at lunch, had a bowl of cereal,
wrote you a letter that I thought might hold with yours.
It brought me up to you. I felt good,
took you back to work.
Eighteen Second Language Teachers
being led by three bureaucrats with big salaries.
The leader's the woman who fought our books.
An hour into the afternoon I'm still doing good,
reading your letter, maintaining my posture.
I get a phone call from a friend. I'm called out,
come back relaxed, a sign? They're fine tuning
their good work. I'm looking at your poems
on the letters, looking at the letters you recommend:
S, O, C, I, & (not really a letter), Y, A, and E.
Kevin, I'm a 51 year-old-man. I said,
I have a story. It's in a letter from a friend.
It's from a story called, Letters of Recommendation.
Listen. Count the sentences. *Let's teach this.*
By this time my cup fills completely.
I read your recommendation for "A".
My heart's beating like it was in the dream I had last week
with the underage girl. That teenage girl in my dream, Kevin,
she's me, too. I mean, she is.

A

appears arrogant,
wants to be first, still, if it stands beside itself,
it fills a room with smoke
coffee, introductions, and steps.
Give A its triplet,
slap her on your bumper
and wait, wait. In its long

sound A's Canada's
sweet alternative to huh.

Kevin Miller

Kevin, from the Dream's standpoint,
that was the high point.
Miranda doesn't give a shit about her father's books.
When she says, O brave new world,
she sees those sailors coming down the beach.

✦

LETTERS OF RECOMMENDATION, AFTER KEVIN MILLER,
WRITTEN DURING THE CURRICULUM MEETING
FOR SECOND LANGUAGE STUDENTS, HOLDING THE POET'S EXAMPLES
IN THE LIGHT FOR MY OWN SURVIVAL

K

The straight line is stiff,
almost like a hexagram
from the *I Ching*. Or is it a compass?
And plumbing this page;
something else,
a sound from the belly,
clearing the throat,
making song possible.
Repelling an attack?
The friend to have,
the harshest angel.

B

The explosive consonant.
Lips breaking away
from the full stop after the colon:
the burst giving energy
to the sentence.
The O gets all the press
for its light, but doesn't B

blind the Cyclops?
Twice the light.
Enough eggs for cookies.

J

is a great letter to pick up
in an old drawer of type.
In the right font
you'd drive out to the point
where the seraph
makes a turnaround and park.
It's a brand on horses.
Are horses slaves, like dogs?
Forgive me. The J
makes a balance
every village needs.
Don't let the rich
zone themselves
into the seraph.

L

My daughter's name
begins here, but this isn't nepotism.
It's a boomerang,
a letter from down under.
The forces of all that's underneath
tuck themselves neatly
into these straight lines.
If you think L
follows company policy,
watch out. Hire someone
you can trust.
Get a Looker. Hire A.

I

Sounds different in Spanish.
Even a different word.
What sounds so noble,
the standing man in a crowd.

I turns into Romeo
on the street,
Yo, Babe. It's me.
A calling from the dark.
If this one doesn't make it
we all go down.
Every time I embrace her
she turns into someone else.

F

This one's Ishmael
in any culture.
Takes the hit
for everything
that can't be said,
for everything
that goes down.
The school's excuse.
Society's outrage.
Men build prisons for F
to protect their women.
Ask the women
about this one.

G

The American teenager
in the suburbs.
Clothes, car, license.
Good curves.
Inside, outside.
Seraphs.
Money for music.
The idol of the world.
But listen to it talk.
Is that a cigarette
hanging from its mouth?

X

Christians wonder about you

looking at this one.
In Chinese the lines
wouldn't be crossed.
You wouldn't know.
Danger. Opportunity.
You can only go one way.
Two of these is a Mexican beer.

O

—*Olive on a toothpick.*
Kevin Miller

Divine song within.
Everything that sings
before the railroad.
Orpheus.
Too much of anything.
The first fall.
The song in a shopping mall.
The porno doll in cellophane.
Christmas wreath in a summer garden.
The tunnel that outlasts the oxygen.
Everything that must be lost.
The snake eating its own tail.
A pipe.
Smoke coming from the fire circle.
Twins. Exclamation and ecstasy.
A young girl at a circus.
The Mandala.
A ring of volcanoes.
Nurturing movement of the Earth.
Magic circle.
The still center.
Round table of oneself.
At last.

•

WAITING WITH MEN, BEING WITH WOMEN

This mutating hybrid we call the present.

What sustains you?—Jim Heynen

The freedom songs of Bob Marley
Lacy Dreamwalker
The evanescence of Karen
Kevin's letters
Wearing the jewelry of Marty Lovins
Reading poems to Grimes
Karen
Rompiendo las cadenas
Pedro Hernandez asking any question
Cutting flowers for women
The dream of the oatmeal cookie
Yoshimi and Alma
The kitchen
Karen's dreams
Lucia and Guadalupe
The Poetry Pole in the Garden
Siendo abrecaminos
Responding to all I've been given
Javier reading
This house, this morning
Janeen
The path of the mailman
My children carrying their own story
The curiosity of María Muniz
Making Karen Latte
The Revolutionary Nature of Dreams
Having Grimes for a friend
Buscando América
Working on books with Karen
Trusting this poem
Being on lookout
Talking with men
Coffee
The women in my life
The large heart

✦

THROWING FRISBEE

All this time, the Dreamwalker
waited for me, tolerated the leash,

allowed me, encouraged me, even,
to teach her to heal. She gave me

signs, too. When we'd drive out
to the Reservation, and I'd cut

her loose, she always returned,
an athlete, through the sage,

graceful, full of herself, for me.
She knew the frisbee was a bird

before I threw it. My friends
knew, too. *Are you and that lab*

still going to school? The chain
snapped each time they spoke.

They are hunters, I told myself.
What their dogs retrieve is dead.

Lacy is a go-between.
She travels the wilderness

of the borderworlds. She's called
to bring back what is ours. Lacy

teaches me more than patience,
waiting for me to throw the

frisbee that first time. She shows
me the dream on the run—

Beautiful thing! Black Lab
at full speed, bird dog, cut loose

from the leash, giving all

for the bird in me.

•

THE REVOLUTIONARY DREAM

One day cashing a check
the checker asks you for your

driver's license. *Do you know*
this license is expired, she says,

looking in my eyes, *You better*
watch out. Driving home

with the groceries, the man
knows he has been dreaming.

He wonders if it's too late
to get it renewed. He wonders

if it's too early to get it renewed.
That night he dreams again.

He is at a river in Chicago,
surrounded by midwest

skyscrapers. On Sunday
the local paper ran a story

on the coyote. Coyote trappers
say two things will survive

the holocaust: cockroaches
and coyotes. A young man

in the dream has been arrested
for taking drugs and must

listen to his accusers. I am one
of them. I stand, shake his hand,

give him my name. I tell him

I made the first call on his house

of cards. Driving home I count
the months I have been driving

around this town without a permit.
Almost a year. The young man

has a rotting front tooth.
Someone tells me to be careful.

I ask the young man if he knows
my son. I tell him I made the call

once before, on my son. The coyote,
swift and efficient, lives on the fringe,

with an appetite for cats and small dogs.
The young man drops his mask,

says, *Tim Bodeen,* and walks off
with my son. My friend Barry Grimes

walks over to me. We walk away.
Homeowners blame the coyote

for their lost pets. One thing,
their pets have disappeared

and there isn't any evidence.
I tell myself to look both ways,

put on my signal to change lanes.
Checking the rear view mirror,

I know the dream has turned
my world upside down, and wonder,

knowing. I could have missed
all this. I could have.

THIS MORNING IN THE WILLIAM STAFFORD ROOM

The computer dictionary wants
to change Asshole to Achilleus,

William Stafford. In another room,
years ago, a woman asked you

a question about the brutes. No,
you said, We don't run from what is.

You were saying, Be brave,
in the dark light. The brutalities

are pointing us toward a truth
we're just beginning to see. Stand

aside. It is only prose standing
in the doorway. The wonders

on the other side are open.
The dream keeps knocking out

all walls, any barriers. The fact
of the door frame is an image

given to us by Adrienne Rich.
Let it stand until its time comes.

Last night I heard a woman
tell how it is to give the question

to children. She shows him
a picture of his blue dog.

She teaches him to read,
The dog is blue, and then,

tender brutality, she marks him,
Is your dog blue? *Is he really?*

Bill, we do this knowing.
The dog may never return.

The boy may grow up
to be a senator. I see you,

holding your arms like a tree,
different things, *Nowhere now,*

you call through every storm,
a voice that wanders without a home.

The new dictionary wants changes.
It wants to turn Ishmael into fishmeal,

calls Orpheus, orphan. Oh, Bill,
the world is Grandfather short.

A young woman looks at a photo
of Lou Costello taped to my notebook.

She wants to know who he is.
Did you know he's from Paterson?

They put up a statue in the park.
Nothing for Williams. Bill,

Who's on first? Can you see
the puzzled look on the child's face,

wanting a dog that will never be blue?
The mandala is a mandate. I'm for that.

You become a staff to become
the world ringing everywhere.

•

Once you get into this room
you never want to leave, look around.

◆

You don't   have any rhythm

at all, Bodeen.

Not fair, Eva Siddhartha Valdivia, Not fair.

Yo enseño a los que no tienen ritmo, a bailar.

Oh, sí. Pero no. I'm way ahead of you, Bodeen.

I've been teaching the men to dance for a long time.

Try the mole. Es mole de mi mamá.

Did you help in the kitchen?

Mole comes from the Aztecas, Bodeen.

Did you use Chocolate Mexicano?

Ceviche, tostadas, pozole, tamales, horchatta.

The mole is not more important than the tortilla.

Come este atole con los tamales.

Banda Maguey, Banda Machos

Reviviendo momentos que vivieron en México.

¿Quién trajo el agua de arroz?

Come on Arizbeth, let's show these boys how to dance.

Bodeen put your hands in the air.

Enchiladas con queso.

You look like you're playing the drums.

Dancing without rest for the first time.

The new culture will come from the ashes of this one.

Tapping feet, ceviche,

Gabachos getting to know who we are.

Juan Arévalo asking for Snoop Doggy Dogg and Tupac and Bone.

Lots of skippers trying to get to our party.

I'm sorry I couldn't dance—it wasn't that I

        didn't want to—it is forbidden me now.

        My Grandmother's death. Estoy de Luto.

The aroma from the food! *¿Quién soy?*

The fish gets cooked in the limón y cebolla.

Gavicel, to dance with Eliseo.

Me dio gusta, Bodeen, que estuvo bailando todo el tiempo.

We can't just save ourselves compartiendo la felicidad.

Somebody go wash these pinche tenedores de plásticos.

We're going to have to help the Gabachos cross this time.

Everybody put your hands in the air.

Pretend to fall down como borachin.

I need a job. ¿Ya hablaste con Phil?

All the laughing people.

"I'm going to take us up the steps of Jerusalem."

"12 Steps from the base to the top."

"The Pyramid game. I'll keep it simple."

"Oh, God, Jim."

"Watch what happens, here."

✦

"PLANT HER OWL EYES"—Gavicel Antúñez

[The Aztecs have two words for soul. Not just one.
The tonal is what we call the alma, the soul.
The nagual is the plant or animal in the exterior world
that functions like the tonal.]

"Siempre soñaba que venía
en los Estados Unidos y ahora es todo una realidad,
y lo siento como si fuera NAHUATL porque
es lo que siento y que seha convertido en realidad.

The owl and Ultima. The nagual and the dream.
Bless me, Anaya, Bendíceme, Ultima...
Curandera, shaman, machi, beauty mingled
with sadness. His soul like the stream

of time. Eliodoro's nagual is the rattlesnake.
Cascabel. I used the víbora para remedio
para quitarme las espinillas de la cara
y para que se limpie, and I believe

in that remedy. I used it. It works.
First I kill him. Y le quito el cuero
y lo pongo a secar luego me como
su carne en comida, o sola. We fear

with my family in my culture. The fact
is evil just because we don't know.

My nagual is my art. I found myself
repeating after her. Dig out the plant,

Oregano is not only a spice, it's a cure
for coughs and fever. My mom helps me
with my dreams. They are not in the future.
They exist now, para mi, la identidad.

My nagual is a bear that I have in me
now and forever. My experience
of being Mexican takes me to that place.
Mariposas en mi corazón—

I know you can get into a different world,
you know what I'm talking about.
If there is despair in your heart, look
for the owls. My father wants me

to work in the bank. The owl is a spirit.
Dreams are a whole different life.
I once dreamed high in the mountains.
Rompecabezas. Innocence keeps

you pure. But at the same time
keeps you naive. Some act naive
all their lives. The owl is Ultima's
shadow taking care of the Curandera.

•

My México, cuando
te abandonaba
me llevaba mi corazón
destrozado,
pero te abandonaba
por alcanzar mis sueños.
Pero tenía
la esperanza de regresar
algún día más preparado—
Para ayudar a mi México.
But llevo tú nombre
muy alto y con mucho orgullo.

My México.

Guadalupe Hernández
Nació en Aranza, Michoacán

•

THE VOICE IN THE DREAM

—The Dream Speaks

My friend and I are on the railroad—

Gale Marquett—

and we're delivering packages,

but I can't tell what kind.

At one point we were riding in a strange car—

open and closed at the same time,

on the rails themselves.

And we're taking showers,

taking turns getting naked,

and brushing our teeth.

Next thing I know

THE WELLS FARGO MAN HIMSELF,

takes a package from us—don't know what,

we're getting off this railroad car

somewhere in some city—
and the Wells Fargo man is angry,

I ignore his anger, then

ignore another comment by a man on the street,

and make a joke of my own seeing some

bottles of Heinz 57 Steak Sauce,

I see you collect those wine bottles,

But the Wells Fargo man,

the son-of-a-bitch is mad. Christ Almighty mad.

He clips my sleeping bag

to my tent, and it ends up getting torn up.

I mean, torn up, which only makes him rage on all the more.

I try and talk to him about his anger.

HE EXPLODES!

I know this about what happens next.

I say to Marquett.

Going home, we're taking an alternative boat,

and we're taking it slow. Now, next thing I know,

I'm home.

Carpenters are in the house,

our house, in the computer room, where Karen and I make books.

AND THEY'RE REMODELING. A man and a woman.

An elaborate frame

built over the doorway.

Karen comes home. I show her the mess.

Putting up a piece of molding

The woman hammers away using ROOFING NAILS

instead of FINISHING NAILS—

bending every other one.

What are you doing? I ask,

I walk through the house   Barry's in the room   with Karen,

Barry screaming at her

about the mess   when the voice comes,

this is   *THE VOICE*   *OF THE DREAM ITSELF,*

THE DREAM IS SPEAKING,

Stop the construction,   Stop the construction.

The voice of the dream wakes me.

✦

The Wells Fargo Man was angry.
He tore things up. My sleeping bag
and tent shredded. But mad
as he was, he wasn't pissed off enough
to wake me from that dream,
so the dream kept going,
the dream came right into my house,
right to the door
where Karen and I make them books.
The dream put a man and a woman
in there with all that scaffolding
around the door frame. And the woman
putting up the molding
with those roofing nails.

And bending those nails, sinking them
deep into the wood with her hammer blows.
What a mess.
And I almost walked out on that, too.
I asked her, You going to leave
those bent nails? I tell Karen,
and Karen looks around, and still,
still, I'm sleeping through this dream.
Finally the Big Unit himself arrives.
Grimes shows up, starts talking to Karen
about this mess in the computer room.
And he can get mad. He'll teach the Wells Fargo guy
about anger. And still I don't wake up.
It takes the voice of the dream itself.
It takes the voice of the dream to get my attention.
Stop the Construction, the dream says.
Stop the construction. I woke up then.
I sat up in bed. I got right up.
I follow orders. I wrote the letter.
I stopped what the dream asked me to stop.
When the dream speaks, I listen.

✦

HOW IT IS THAT LUIS VASQUEZ BECOMES THE NAGUAL OF THE CROW

When I was a little boy my first pet was a crow.
I found it under a big coconut tree in El Salvador.
The bird was almost dead, so I took it home to cure it.
Weeks passed and the bird got healthy.
I was about ten years old. No one wanted me to keep it.
Not even my Mom. She said,
Those birds only bring mala suerte.
I wouldn't believe that. My abuelita told me,
M'ijo, I'm going to tell you a little story about those birds.
Those birds carry your soul when they die.
Part of your soul will go away,
so don't give all your love to it.
But I didn't care about what she said.
My father yelled at me,
You let the bird fly, or I'll whip you te voy a chingar

if you don't listen. —Yes, I said,
so I'll get it out of the cage. The bird flew away.
I cried, too. But the bird never left.
It was around the house peeking in on me,
and always I'd go for a walk, and the bird
came to me and steps on my shoulder.
I named the bird, Oscuro, a word
that is like the shadow. I was so happy
to have the bird with me. One day Papa said,
El pájaro que éste trajo a la casa
only brought bad luck to all.
So the bird escaped in branches of the tree
by the window and disappeared.
I looked out and I saw it dead with a slingshot.
The bird was dead. And it's true,
with the bird, part of my life went away,
my childhood became sad and the image
of my dead bird came to me very often.

Then I had this dream.
It was one of the most nice dreams I ever had.
My dream was about my crow that died.
I dreamed that I died,
and in the other side, a wonderful place,
someone told me, You must go back to earth,
but not as a human, as a bird.
The dream was long ago.
Suddenly I was down there,
my body covered with *plumas.*
I flew with a flock of crows,
seeing people making bad things to the other.
So I had the power of punishing them all.
All the bad people.
That dream was special to me.
With just a look I gave to the bad people,
they feel *dolor* and regret
of what they'd done to others.

When I woke up
I thought of the words my grandma
had said once to me, *that bird still carried my soul.*
I was scared and happy at the same time.

'Cause for just a moment I could make bad people
pay for what they had done to innocent ones.

•

ON THIS PATH, THROUGH THIS HOUSE

I sit up in bed. I am on an island
in another man's house, surrounded

by water. I write down the notes
from my dream. There has been

a shipwreck. I am with friends,
the men I hike with. I plant a garden

in the holes of a raft. I have used
another man's electricity.

I want to remain on this island,
and I want to get off of it, too.

A man and a woman find us.
It is their house. They row

here in a 2 man boat, one carved
by hand like in the old days.

They discovered the electricity.
I put down the pen. Karen turns

to me in the bed. She picks up the pen
and starts writing. Dazed

by my dream already, dazed
now by Karen, I watch her write,

Key Lime Pie, funeral,
buried with husband—

people need permission.
Walking to the shower I know

Karen will tell me her dream
and I will listen.

BOOK FOUR

The Garden Gate

...it was a point of honor to have no bias regarding outcome.

—Louise Glück

Book Four

THE GARDEN GATE

Just love.

Just that.

✦

THE GARDEN GATE

Same stained cedar gate we opened
25 years ago to bring in an old refrigerator,
rebuilt by John Greer, the Irish carpenter,
to add a latch. Pushing too hard to get it open December 31,
rushing to hold off the water coming from the roof,
between the roof and the basement, shoveling snow,
breaking ice on the roof with an ax,
the broken gate turns into the only casualty of the winter storm.
This gate, by John Greer, the Irishman,
who set the press, added on our deck and kitchen,
is framed and rebuilt around an old bed frame.

Six screws, each its own size, three Phillips head,
three standard, plus the latch, come out to replace
the broken board. My only substitution is pine for cedar,
thinking to gain strength. I measure, use a drill.
I trace my steps. But can I get those screws
back in the same holes into that steel bed frame?
The old fashioned latch is for appearance only.
This is something neighbors figure out.
Watching me throughout the afternoon,
Karen comes out to hold the board and says, Wire it.

•

—Morning Lines For Jim Heynen

Wish me success. Wish us success.

My friend includes me in his work.
His work becomes these lines.

He must talk to one of the bright young men.

One who can pay the tuition.
One whose judgment and sarcasm is a poison.

I am going to try a loving firm confrontation.

I feel included without having to listen.

I know what this bright young man feels like.

He is carrying poison.
I have been trained to deny it.
I have eaten it in my efforts to be kind
and it has killed me.

His poison is poison. I tell my friend this.

Poison doesn't take it personal. Poison treats everybody the same.

You're only a man.

•

AFTER THE DREAM

Stuff that's carried us.

The train is rigid, but it's also fate.

The shower in the open car is great.

You're cleansed, you're exposed.

If you go to the roots and clean up again,

then what happens?

Oh, those railroad tracks.

I grew up on those tracks.

Walking rails is how I learned to play and balance.

It's where I learned to be alone.

If you know the territory you can go to the heart.

What makes it difficult to deal with poison

is when we don't know the poison in ourselves.

✦

SONG LIGHT

–for Rob Prout

The heart of the photograph,

my friend says. *I took these images*

I hadn't been able to use. The art of cropping.

Looking at the Palimpsest Wall, poems, and photos

held by masking tape, in story light

this morning, it's clear: *Rob's father is dying.*

Jackie has time to complete the new quilt

to help him make

safe passage. He's already broken free—

he's had his son back—

These three years in Yakima,

with his son,

have delivered him—

Everything he planted in Texas,

blooming in the rich, irrigated Yakima Valley,

—Seems just yesterday it was a desert, too!

There is always a photo underneath the photo.

The image emerging from a silver past

to another generation of nonbelievers—

Nothing is lost, No one ever dies.

The art of cropping can be learned

by drawing a circle in the sand.

All I ever have to do is pay attention.

My friend tells me everything.

Each time he looks at me

he gives me what he has to give.

He is a photographer.

The other morning, asking about my wife,

how she's doing, what's happening with her computer

he was telling me his life story then,

taking photos of his father, remembering him,

calling him up on the screen,

bringing him here from Texas,

calling him home, coming home himself,

thumbing through the family album,

Father, father.

✦

And I saw a light that took a river's form—
—Dante, Paradiso, Canto XXX, 61

I hadn't read from here
since the year I walked
with Dante every day.
This is what it's like to walk alone.

✦

WORKING FOR THE POEM WITH THE BOOKSELLERS

or is it, marriage? *Beautiful thing.*

Karen and I wake up Sunday morning
in a hotel room
in Spokane

Beautiful thing, an alarm buzzing

interrupts my dream

Somebody's trying to learn Spanish

and get it right   We're in a hotel room   in Spokane

Working for poetry

This weekend started
way last week
making the catalogue right
naming our poets
cutting and pasting
on the kitchen table
like the old days

old farts
showing the kids
one more time
how to have fun

Karen and I
Beatrice on the bed table
Karen snoring in the bed itself
Cordelia saying, *No cause, no cause*

Working for the poem

interrupts spring and all
it's the Ides of March
A four hour drive
We're in a snow storm
on Saint Paddie's Day
Kids from school bands
in uniforms step into the hotel
to get out of the weather

Long marriage!

Asphodel,

even as I reach out to rub your back,

I feel that knot

You're here in this room

On this path, through this house

Beautiful thing!

We set up a table for poetry

in the middle of the city
we have business cards
with our names
This is literature
that means business
Not for sale
The poem is part of the gift
an exchange of vows

You can have the book, lady—
but that don't make it a gift exchange!

Karen's got these people around her
in a room full of books
A book show, featuring,

America,
We're a table set with real food
The bonsai book
can teach you lots, and the illustrations
in those bird books were lovely
the dictionaries straighten us,

—Notice all the root words gone?

The new dictionary censors itself
to make a sale
Like our lives never happened

Karen's talking to two angels

they find her in this room!

They pick her from this *fracaso* of a culture

The woman wants to know why we do the poem

Asphodel,
It's a free gift

that greeny flower,
Your husband is a minister for Christ
you know the cost
You gotta give to the muse
to get something back

If you want to learn
to write the poem
All poems are spiritual, for Christ's sake,
you have to leave the village behind—
Hopkins, can put Jesus in his poems
because it cost him all he had
beautiful thing

God isn't saying whose side he's on
You want to write the poem
You gotta give it up
and find out what your dream says
and do that—
It's been a long apprenticeship

You want to write the Christian poem
you got to leave the village church
and that means the language, too,
got to leave it behind. It means,
and I say this because you asked,
probably your village husband, too

You already know this

You left him years ago

The Angels

You angels

Waiting for us all the time

We just don't know it

My dream said, Stop the construction!
My dream adopted me

All my teeth fall out in my dream
All my masks are down
I saw my son walk off with a man
whose tooth was broken,
he had greasy hair—
I stayed behind in a suit of clothes
I think maybe that man was Christ
Maybe Dionysus
I don't know yet

I have to wait for more information

Even the language is dead

Break words free

Not one Canto in this room, not one

No Williams, No Rexroth, No Rukeyser

Not a single book will enter Barnes & Noble without a Bar Code

You should've seen us,

Karen and me, Thursday night Getting ready

Mr. and Mrs. Tom Paine
working on two computers
Writing copy
Doing layout
A flurry of energy
Exchanging discs
Exhausted after day jobs
This is poetry not marketing
What the muse demands
Call her up on the screen
The imagination

I come home from work
I can't take the Dreamwalker to this show
I don't want to leave my pup behind
I already let go of my kids

Karen's talking to me
about the FBI
They got an informant says
there's going to be a holdup—
A bank robbery!
Monday morning
they're bringing in a SWAT team
I have to be in the basement
This is no dream, Jim,
He's been planning this for weeks
I'm going to let them in
They want to take him
when he puts his hand
on the door He's planning
on spray painting the cameras
The FBI's going to call
Sunday night when we get home

Karen's carrying this to Spokane
to the bookfair

Karen's talking to the FBI
And I'm taking her to a book show
Going to make her stand up for poetry
in a roomful of suits

A man watching TV

You think I'm making this up

I come, my love, to sing to you.

For the adventures
in the little books
are more than enough

The Valkyries, the food, The young Jewish woman,

Beautiful thing!
Sleep all morning
We got this hotel key until noon

But one of your daughters will call
I'll bet so

From Ellensburg,
From Mexico,
to check in
to make sure
you're there

Beautiful thing

They still see by your light

Home Sunday night, tired,

waiting for the FBI to call

the phone rings   it's him,

Karen listening,   checking off

ok,   ok,   ok,   ok,

Karen saying, *There's somebody else on the line,*

the FBI man saying, it's probably

my kids downstairs

•

LINES FOR ZEV FROM THIS MOVIE

a woman's world,
of crossed sticks,

Show the young man those lines, Zev.
It's all film, nothing is lost—
Francisco comes
into my room with his pictures of this weekend,
La Migra walking into the warehouse
where his mother works, rounding up 49 people,

taking one of my cousins, they put them
in the lunch room, papers or not,
and bussed them to Seattle, no time
for clothes, money. The owner called
my grandmother, he'd heard, told her
to stay home, the pastor at St. Joseph's
gave four services while the *migra* waits
out front, and finally we leave the church
through the back door, they're just using us,
they took some kids from Selah High School,
would our school let them take us?
Donde hubo fuego cenizas quedan,
When there is fire, ashes remain,
the worst thing you can do is panic,
my mother's patron put up a ladder
to the attic, una escalera, you know,
and they all climb into the roof...

I save everything my friend gives me
from his daughter's dreams. Miriam,
in a dream you can talk to rocks. Miriam,
a dream is a great pretend. Miriam,
last night all the log houses over the ocean
collapsed. Children rolled into the sea
leaving their bicycles. The bicycles
are gone. The boys drinking from 6-ounce
cans of Olympia beer don't see a thing.
I am with them drinking tomato juice.
Entire buildings. Remember Lincoln Logs?
Remember the music they make falling
into each other? This is what it's like
and I am one of the boys
evacuating from a collapsing community.
A sheet of plastic separates us from the ocean.
We cut through it with scissors,
binding ourselves to remnants of old houses,
these fallen logs, cut down to our size, our new boats.

Karen's in the bank basement this minute
with two FBI men. A SWAT team of five hides
across the street. This is the second morning
to wait. The informant says it's today.

He's going to try and take the manager
when she opens the door. She knows him,
He grew up with her son. He plans to take her
at the door, spray paint the cameras.
The manager can't tell her husband.
Doesn't think he can take it.
She wants to call the young felon on the phone.

During the last fifteen minutes of the book fair
a woman stops at the Blue Begonia table.
How much is that book? She is looking at one lone copy
of Al Het, for the sins, the smallest book in the show.
I tell her that it's hers, that I was waiting for her
to claim it. I really like saying this.
Michele Yanow from the Tree of Life
knows these poems come from a faraway story.
She reads the five poems, asking,
What is the cost of this book?
I show her my notebook.
I show her the photo of your hand holding
my copy of Paterson, cut and pasted on my notebook
the day we went to the falls. Your watch shows noon.
I show her Zev Shanken reading in Paterson
over the falls by the Williams River.

Dan Peters leaves work. It's like this, he says,
giving me a sheet of paper. Like this.
One morning, two busses, one night.
He is trying to get to work and finds himself
alongside a white DOJ-INS Deportation bus.
Blue Bird logo painted green.
Green chevron tilted sideways pointing forward.
Empty seats. White metal screens on the windows.
An agent stands in the stairwell.
In front of him is a school bus. Regulation.
Blue and yellow. Blue Bird.
I'm off the hook. I'm not on either bus.
Rattlesnake Hills and Toppenish Ridge.
Lower Valley sky. Northeast clouds.
Fir, sage, brine, disked earth.
Notes brought to me from the external world.
A young man moves into his life and vanishes.

Maybe one dream in four to talk about.
The richest man in the world.
What happens if I break just one chain?
Who is that man breaking into the bank?
Who is that guy?
Javier says, The only fear I have
is the fear my mother gives me.
She carries the entire culture, Javier!
Small wonder! You're looking
into the heart of a 1000 year old pueblo.
Cindy García says her mother got her papers
two years ago but it didn't make no difference.
Her mother laughed and they took her downtown.
Which part of the dream is the dream?
When we have better stories
our choice is to speak or remain silent.

One side of your ticket admits you to the dream.
One side of your ticket gets you into the clubhouse.

•

Before the garden gate, but not in the garden.
What is it between the spare relic and the body?

The ice, the melt, subterranean, yet whole.
Stressful, guarding against the loss.

•

Nike. And storms.

    Nike.

Greek Goddess of Victory, loose in America
    another unknown,
    Eunice, Nicholas (nickel), Nike

I've got to get this out. Stay out of the paper.
    Stay on the path.

"We do not want to become an oasis

for those people who would just rather stay on welfare,"
explained state Senator Alex Deccio, R-Yakima,
a key architect of the GOP reforms."

Nike.

Last year the Victory Goddess raked in 680 million in profits.

Does it sell cigarettes? No, shoes to teenagers and universities.

And the Swoosh—

A logo—not a symbol.

✦

The counter stress.

Karen says, I don't like
the way you change facts.

"It was the love of love,
the love that swallows up all else,
a grateful love"

✦

Like pollen,
Like the nose of the puppy.

That fast.

Turning away from the garden—
with the hand already on the gate.

✦

MOVING OUTSIDE

–for Roland Dougherty

With music, too big, too soon.
In one night, the moon's eclipse

in the east, the bright comet
roaring west. And now, the sun,

young shoots, the human voice,
and drums. The Poetry Pole.

Delphiniums coming through
unraked leaves, a Bachelor Button

in the roses. New songs from Van—
everything that used to be:

This used to be my life.
Play the rake. Tap the shovel.

⬩

"We friends" or "People like us"
is how they refer to themselves.

He who tastes, knows,
not by argument—love

makes the difference,
not ascetics, not mind.

Rumi. Graves. Shaw.
Absorption leads to ecstasy—

Live love practically.
All Sufis know this.

⬩

A shard of glass, an arrowhead
into a tire built to cover

60,000 miles. The Goodyear Man
in a suit, telling me,

One revolution breaks the radial.
On the corner where my students

walk back to the barrio.
You teach those guys,

I feel sorry for you.
Don't feel sorry for me.

✦

Somos mojados, Maestro,
Javier's mother tells me

at Albertson's. Witness
the death of a friend.

A man bent on taking
everyone down.

A woman meets me at my door.
With coffee. I'm slow to catch on,

a dream in her hand, gone.
You'll do something.

I'll be with my father
when he dies. I'll be there.

✦

But what of theme? Except
by the effect on the reader?

If they still have validity,
they confirm the intuition

of the Welsh poet Alun Lewis
just before his death:

the *single* theme,
Life & Death, &

what survives of
the Beloved. Robert Graves

on Majorca, at 65,
the fox who lost his brush,

nobody's servant,
only poetry into poems,

from nests lodged in rock clefts,
built of carefully chosen twigs,

perfect faithfulness,
between delight and horror,

lined with white horse hair,
plumage of prophetic birds.

The Theme: Antique story.
Birth, life, death,

resurrection of the God
of the Waxing Year,

the God's losing battle
with the Waning Year

for love of the Goddess,
mother, bride, layer-out.

The poet identifies
with the Waxing Year,

his Muse with the Goddess.
His rival is his blood-brother,

his other self, his weird,
often appearing

in his Night Mare
as Prince of Air.

•

I wave goodby

to the Waterman.

Why? he asks,
intimating division

remaining in the dream.
The adventure brings me

closer to her. Farewell.
Go on, in Goodby.

I feel the Goddess
but can't see her.

Nothing on earth
is more contemptible

than borders. *Las fronteras*
no existen. I dream

to be a man at home
in this house, walking

through endless rooms,
building and leaving.

✦

Javier tells the women
but he doesn't tell me—

he'll marry for papers,
he'll marry to stay.

Key provisions in the law
taking effect Tuesday

makes it easier to deport
illegal aliens. May the light

whose name is Splendor
refer to vision, not the Sun.

Crossing the border
changes one para siempre,

I know that. I carried
Paz on a trail below Patoo

years ago, seeing the word
opens my exile.

•

American standards.
The left hand curls around

the slide trombone, holding
position. A boy from a remote

village is taken up by sound,
and a mouthpiece so cool

to the touch no translation is made,
only initiates. *That sound,*

Mama, that sound, that's what
I'm listening for. Funny valentine,

is a memory of brusque downtime,
wobbly blats, slurs, wind tones.

This crooning is a dialogue
with a past the boy had no access to,

the twenties and thirties arriving
to the snow-swept prairies, coal furnace

raging through a cold house.
Layers and layers of music.

•

Help me.

✦

Help me.

✦

I wasn't ready
when I wasn't called.

What happened?

Not even a no.
Nothing.

Over and over.
What was so different?

I can say it
this morning.

Why did I get hit so hard?
My mind played every game.

True poets in olden days
must solve a riddle.

Rejection in its most pure form.
At the most base level.

Open what is shut.
Shut what is open.

✦

Help me write the poem.

✦

Pruning in the roses
Van singing,

No more heroes,

reduced to zeroes

when that rough God
goes riding, riding on in.

✦

FOR THE PHOTOGRAPHER BEFORE THE DOOR; NOTES FROM ROBERT GRAVES

Latins worshipped
the White Goddess
as *Cardea*, and Ovid
tells a muddled story

connecting her
with the word, *Cardo*,
a hinge. She loved
Janus, two-headed

god of doors,
and the first month,
and had charge
of the hinges.

She protected infants
against witches
from cradles.
Ovid tells it

inside out.
Cardea was *Alphito*,
who destroyed children
after disguising herself—

Janus, stout guardian,
kept her out. But before
Janus, he was her son,
and she was White Goddess,

Cardea. And though
he became the Door,

national guardian,
she became the hinge,

connecting him
to Door-post .
Cardo, the hinge,
is *cerdo*, craftsman,

She must keep out
her crafty self.
Ovid says,
her power casts spells

with the hawthorn,
the religious formula:
to open what is shut,
shut what is open.

✦

Dull-white leprosy
Quick as a flash
Nurse to infant Dionysus
Argo, famous dog of Odysseus

✦

To be delivered
by invocation and prayer

I arose with a joyful face
plunged my head 7 times in water

Blessed woman,
original source

grant me thy food,
the acorn, of olden time

nourish all seeds
by thy damp heat

by your feminine light
according to the wanderings

of the sun
near and far

end my fallen hopes
deliver me from wretched fortune

Queen of all in Hell
Deliver us, deliver me.

✦

The roses are pruned.
Cut the losses in the heart.

✦

A night battle.
An army overrun.

When it's time
to get out

I discover
I have no shoes.

Laces tight.
Taking the time

to loosen them,
an enemy officer

at my side
tells me not

to bother,
to go barefoot.

✦

APRIL 2, 1997

A sweeping immigration reform law
designed to shore up U.S. borders
and expedite deportations took effect
at 35 minutes past midnight on Tuesday

after judges, lawyers, and advocates
battled into the night over implementation.
Immigrants across the nation
awoke baffled and scared. *No truth*

to the rumor and falsehood that INS
has planned and defined massive deportation
proceedings, says INS spokesman Brian Jordan.
This is going to be a gradual process.

It's going to take time. The law paves the way
for physical barriers at the borders—
including a triple fence at San Diego,
limitations on legal challenges.

✦

THE JOURNEY HOME

Starts with me asking Sergio for a word
to call the *cabroncito* on the other side of the room,
a name that wouldn't start a war with *Raza.*
He gives me *chapetas,* rosy cheeks,

and Fabiola explodes. She has a better word.
We are on edge. These words all come from
our mothers. And our mothers have been
taken from us at an early age. Fabiola's mother

left her in Michoacán to come North,
lost to her before she came to any school.
Now the mothers are put on busses again,
this time taken back the other way—where

is home? *Cuando lleguemos.* No wonder
our humor is so tough. On our journey
we never arrive—*nunca llegamos.* The mother
wears black rubber boots when she crosses

the border into Mexico. *This is a news story.*
Her ankles are chafed where the boots
pinched from the leg chains. Cd. Juarez.
One of 38 workers arrested during the raid

at the Sunnyside Food Plant. First,
she must cut the chains. Then she begins
her journey home to the Yakima Valley.
Remaining in Mexico is not an option—

I can't leave my children, she says,
in the Sunday paper. David Gutiérrez
told us the story the day it happened.
She takes a bus to Nogales where she

can get a passport. She travels with a man
who works with her—they earn $8.60 an hour
stacking cans on an assembly line—
they continue by bus to Tijuana, where

the *coyote* guides them across the border.
Not all coyotes are dangerous, some are angels.
But they're expensive, $1000 each to cross.
They hike for two days to San Diego

where another coyote takes them to L.A.
and a bus to Yakima. *We Mexicans have words*
for everything and we want them used right,
Francisco tells me. A cabrón *is a goat*

you know, but it's not. It's a guy who's always
fooling around. Fabiola knew Sergio was wrong.
Las Perreras, that's the INS car, but it's not.
A perrera is the truck with the dog cages.

✦

ABOUT THE INS—The Federal Immigration and Naturalization Service

Has a current budget of 3.1 billion up from 1.5 billion in 1993.
Nationwide, INS deported 68,000 people last year.
The INS deported 4,881 people from Washington state last year.
About 60 percent of those deported were from Eastern Washington.
The cost of deporting one person ranges
from a few hundred to several thousand, depending.
Deportees are transported by a bus system operated by INS.
West Coast Transportation System runs 27 busses in six western states.
A bus departs from Seattle every Monday, Tuesday, Wednesday.
The INS also uses airplanes. All deportees by air are kept in shackles.
The INS office in Yakima currently has a staff of 28 people.
In 1992 the office was staffed with 12 people.
Along with hiring 1000 new border patrol agents this year,
INS officials have requested adding 156 agents nationwide.
The agency also has requested hiring 422 employees to enhance
its detention and deportation operations.

Source: *Yakima Herald-Republic, A daily part of your life.*

BOOK FIVE

One Path

Yes swells in our souls

Book Five

Call it up from the garden.

I am bringing in saxophones.

I carry a music box in my hand—

                    importation of prayer.

The garden, this garden, full of flowers,

this garden is a resting place for songs.

the poet sings on behalf of all that grows,

                    but I carry the music in my hand,

                    outside myself,

                    exhausted from the dream work,

Become the garden.

•

Dirt from tilled garden beds
works its way into my shoes and socks.
Getting ready. Preparing the way.
Back tired from stretching, pulling weeds,

stored magic in the soil.
Chains of more than coincidence show again—
the poem goes about on its own.

Looking into the press for an ancestor—

Tom McGrath from North Dakota,
waiting for coals to get hot on the grill,
J. J Johnson playing standards Live
at the Village Vanguard, entire schools

compressed into a gesture with the trombone slide,
the other eye, Blake's ecstatic yes, opens
to City Light Howl. Allen Ginsberg is dead.
I am in the garden surrounded by the ancestors.

You stepped out of a dream. Misty.
Every muse poet dies for the Goddess he adores,
ah, Carl while you are not safe, I am not safe,
words mixing with smoke from the fish,

the clear notes of the trombone,
the human voice rocking in the roses,
neighbors listening to this wail,
Allen Ginsberg is with us in Yakima

with the twenty-five thousand mad comrades.
Allen Ginsberg, invoking the muse Walt Whitman,
putting it all on the table in 1950:
It's a great flat plain; we can see everything.

Over and over eating the low root of the Asphodel.
I always wanted to return to the body where I was born.
America when will you take off your clothes?
Jack Kerouac sat beside me on a busted rusty iron pole.

I am given a voice that sends with the smoke while the fish cooks.
I am given a dream where nobody dies.
I am given the halibut to serve with the surfacing poem.
It does not matter if the body is flesh or fish.

•

The translator's sensitivity to the poet's voice
is what draws me to your imagination, Judy.
Bien: es lo que decíamos ahora

Encenderse las lamparas sin motivo aparente.

Retain the conversational tone to project
the irrational image. Not to confuse, no,
exhausted or resting, to serve up
exhaustion or rest. No riddle. The true

poet accepts the mare's nest as life work.
There is no academy in the garden.
Stretched to tears by my own stubbornness,
I howl, *Mule, Mule,* leading myself into silence

for the ancient cycle promising waking and sleeping
in each moment, a life in the beat of a single artery.
You travel the night that will turn into day,
while pretenders, the gleemen of our time,

write the nightmares of our age, the dreams
they've never had, the mare's nest they've never slept in.
The rose has been watered, the bed made,
and the ancient hoe, this garden's only editor,

continues to cull the false from the true
into the language of music. I love the soft voice
of Nela Río becoming harsh. The Argentine woman
writing in Canada travels the length of two continents

for the poem, imagine that! *Mujer, es tu tiempo de relámpago*
y de permanencia. How far she travels, striving,
ivory knuckles knocking, to mirror your work in Bellevue.
I set these lines on the kitchen table, an offering.

•

Lacy Dreamwalker runs with her sister.
Her mother Chrissie teaches her to retrieve in water.
What do they know of each other?
Mother and daughter swimming in competition.

A windswept Alpine doesn't survive the winter.
A community of four tiny firs replace it.
I rebuild the mountain at my doorstep,

a bonsai world on a dramatic path winding

in and out through a mountain pass.
In the sweet embrace of life, it's all garden,
and no garden is safe, not even the refuge.
Where one gives up all there is no path.

A young violinist writes from the city.
A mailman crosses a mountain pass to put it in my hands.
She is going to China. She wonders what happened
to her in Denmark. She remembers throwing

her glasses at the woman in charge,
and Blake speaking for her, *led to believe a lie,*
in her rage. She follows her muse-ic,
watching children at play. Labyrinth

in a cultural game. Friendship and enmity.
Shows of force, forbidden words.
Playing tricks and playing ball.
If you don't master the code,

you're lost. In the child's culture,
all rules are unwritten. The engine
that drives all forms of play is curiosity,
the insatiable heart, venturing from

polished process and forms.
One thinks of the Pentagon.
Child culture needs to break away.
Once you learn to ride a bicycle

the world will never be the same.
As we create, we are created.
Thou shalt play with abandon.
This is life in the garden,

trying to find meaning no matter
how far out, no matter how far off.
The puppy barks. The puppy wants to go.
Pick up a stick and throw.

•

We're at a game, a basketball game.
My wife and my son, and me.
I don't know where the girls are.
But we're driving down Lake City Way,
in Seattle, our first suburb after leaving North Dakota.
Karen is driving. Then Tim. Turning right
at the bottom of the hill towards a classmate
with a knack for finding trouble.
Suddenly Tim has the car going uphill, perpendicular,
and I get mad and take over the driving.

But now,
the car is a sled, and we're entering an old school gym,
and I'm steering the sled over cement blocks
that used to hold up my bookshelves. Even more,
these blocks were placed here by my daughters,
with my help. I check the bottoms of the skis
and they're ruined. Chunks of dried cement
have left cave models of themselves.
These are skis given to me by my son at great sacrifice
now turned into a killing field. This is where
I become aware of the battle. Real warfare.
Rifles. My family is gone. An infantryman
is trying to settle us down. *Get nitrogen to clean*
those guns, he says. *That will keep the barrels clean.*

That's the dream. I embrace it this morning.
I don't mess with my dreams, and I'm grateful.
The man who taught me to dream has let me go on.
Before turning out the light my wife asks me
if I'm going skiing tomorrow. *If I can turn it*
into prayer. I don't know what this means.
I know I'm blessed. I'm in the garden.
I'm outside. The dream still talks to me.
Do not prattle before the people of the path,
the Sufi master Sanai, of Afghanistan wrote.
Sanai was Rumi's teacher.
Who do I thank? *The ordinary man repents his sins.*

The elect repent of their heedlessness.

•

SPRING SKIING IN A STORM AFTER A DREAM

Report the dream.
Be thankful for it.

It is my mother's birthday.
She is at a baseball game.

I am on White Pass,
a solitary.

•

An explosion brings down
an ice wall in the snow movie

at a weekday matinee.
It is the final scene.

This is what it feels like
in the dream, I tell Karen,

This is what it feels like
when the world falls,

such a relief, just like
this ice that no longer

has to hold itself up.

•

The path of waking up
is one path. I no longer

understand the sleepers.
It is all I can say. The path

veers off into trees. Cold
and foggy. A Buddhist

reminds me, all sailors
are condemned

for leaving home.

✦

My blue skis
peek into a storm.

The sun finds my face.
A man writes, It is a great

blessing to lose something
you really want.

This mountain
of snow holds me

and releases me. I ski fast
remembering Allen Ginsberg.

✦

The big run all to myself.
Corn snow softening in a storm.

Put away the poem

and ski. Wake and ski.
She is in the edges,

setting and releasing.
Hide and seek in the moguls.

A man will disappear
in each turn of the skis.

✦

Tips of Alpine Fir
at eye level take me

back to the garden.
Big rocks is a dream

embraced from long hikes
into the wilderness.

It is all wild for the solitary.
The man on the path

dusts himself in snow.
These moss-covered limbs.

✦

A band of light
down a trail above tree line

at noon. I speak
my first words riding a lift

with another man
who asks me about my skis.

Yes, I say, Yes. They are gifts.
I don't tell him where

they take me. He wasn't
asking about my life.

✦

Thighs burning before noon.
Sun and clouds playing shadow

games on the snow field.
What part of the path

is a secret? What part
of the poem must be hidden?

•

I remember when skiing
first saved my life.

Even then, wasn't it Her
bringing me to the poem?

•

It's lunch time.
I have three kinds of fruit.

The juice of the orange
is nothing like the descent.

•

This is about execution.
Below Hourglass I ski

through a community of trees
mirroring the ones I planted

at my front door. I am all rhythm,
dancing between rock and limb.

Before each lift, I push
the ski to get the heartbeat.

•

Released from the ski
at lunch is too sudden.

I'm too free, too warm.
My cheeks get blasted

in the lodge. The orange peel
stings my sunburned lips,

the mustard on the oat bread
seats me in the chair.

Opening the Thermos,
pouring coffee,

I think I have the nose
of a bird dog.

✦

Waking after lunch
with the Sufi book on my lap,

who wouldn't want
to be Rumi?

Isn't this part of the path,
this desire?

✦

Brother David taught me
to say thanks for everything,

but it was Charles Lamb
who first got my attention

with his anger over
the state of Grace—

only before meals,
not before Shakespeare

and other pleasures. Bob Marley's
voice sings to me each ride

on the chair lift, Thank you, Lord,
for what you've done for me.

✦

Now it's about speed.
I'm not executing anything.
Go fast.
I'm too tired to turn.
No edges left.
Skis flat.
This two minute poem.
Glimpse of sun.
Late afternoon, cold day.
Spring below, in town.
Fast.
Go slow in town.

•

DREAMING HER, DREAMING ME

She shows again last night.
And I am afraid.
She's fully grown now.
And charming.
In the sweet embrace of life
dream her back.
Lady of the wild things.

•

LACY DREAMWALKER AND THE DREAM

I was afraid the dreams would leave me.
Lacy can take the frisbee out of the air
at a full sprint. If I can throw it.
She's herself in her coming on.
Lacy's at my feet now.
She has visited me three times, in three ages.
She's gorgeous. She terrifies.
She wants only the charm.
She wants to know what is real.
Lacy Dreamwalker is a theory of writing poems.
There's another dog, too. A white three-legged dog.
The secretary says they're both good dogs.

✦

THE WHITE GODDESS ON WHITE PASS

This morning is about speed.
Snow, icy from last night's freeze.
The trumpet blows
from the back of a pickup in New Orleans.
Open air church. A tailgate platform for Christ.
No *Our Father* here.
Hogback to the South.
The big mountain, white, to the NW.
Everybody's exposed today. No cover.

To see oneself on a field of snow,
alone, no shadows,
and to feel oneself
crossing white space,
the skis turning onto a path
putting one face to face
with Mt. Rainier.
Magical practice.
Meditation, memory, song.

A woman sings.
We say yes.

Now we're alone
with a mountain to sing on.

In a snow cave seated,
and facing Mt. Rainier ,
She Who Shines For All,
back before alphabets, what was,
Irish *ollave* sitting next to the king,
like the queen herself—
dressed in six colors and listening to the wind.

✦

The sweet embrace.

THE ALL-DAY POEM

Coltrane was before God with his saxophone.
Lost people don't understand, sleep through the music.
In the longest riffs he is only waiting for us to catch up.
One day he gives up cigarettes, alcohol and heroin
and steps out of time to make music.
As my wife walks out the door, I say
Find your music, howl a love supreme.
Jack Kerouac puts a roll of paper towels
into a typewriter. Allen Ginsberg calls his friends
sacramental companions, and I run out
to buy a camera to preserve this fleeting moment.
Words before a single drumstick don't disappear.
A hand tapping a rake carries enough of a beat
to keep the breath alive. A word comes from
the reeds. The situation of the west
gets moved about in our binoculars.
Pain and joy in each moment.
Some of us blessed with desire, laugh.

In a vision of Foster's Cafeteria by Robert Levine,
Ginsberg sits where he used to come downstairs and have coffee.
Pure angelic poetry. A united front of angels.
Adopted from prose seeds. Open secrecy.
The new line emerges in liner notes from a reading of Howl.
A musical setting. Ginsberg, Buddhist Jew,
kicked out of Czechoslovakia for corrupting the kids,
the King of May, because he saw Blake in a dream,
teaching us how to write, turning away from Williams
in the Romantic moment. Open secrecy. Musical setting.

Prose seeds. Phrasing. Breath groups.
Towards Hebraic-Melvelian-Bardic.
I thought I wouldn't write a poem but just write
what I wanted to without fear. Open secrecy.
Let my imagination go. Scribble magic lines
from my real mind. Open secrecy. Sum up my life.
I wouldn't be able to show anybody.
Write for my own soul's ear

and a few other golden ears.
But how sustain the long line in poetry
lest it lapse into prosaic? Natural inspiration
of the moment, keeps it moving—
shorthand notation, visual.../
notations of one's own spontaneous phrasing
one after another—at least the ear hears itself—
juxtaposition of hydrogen jukebox—
sustain the mystery. Abstract haiku.
Finally, completely free composition.
Open secrecy. The long line breaking up
itself into short staccato breath units
linked with dashes—
the long line a variable stanza unit
measuring a group of related ideas—
marking them—
ending with a hymn in rhythm
similar to synagogic death chant—
at least the ear hears itself
in Promethean natural measure
not in mechanical count of accents.

✦

I picked asparagus in those fields,
she says. That's how she starts.
Driving in a truck.
Full with music.
A truckful of music.
Telling stories back and forth.
Marsalis.
Wynton Marsalis and his band.
Listen. The sweet embrace.
The story.
Now tell me about you.
The deepest penetration.

✦

Vandals put an orange traffic cone
on the Poetry Pole in the Garden,
and take the Prayer Flags.

Karen says they need them more than I do.
I'm not so sure and drive around town
until I find another orange cone—
they're there—and I exchange the Flags
for the cone, leaving two markers
for the pranksters looking for a path.

✦

The Drum Lady
rides the Conga
belted to her waist.
Fill up your spaces
take it with you.
If you listen
you're going to know
where you're going.

You're going to know
where your part is.

Respect your instruments.

They are your strikers.

Let us get a hold of the downbeat.

✦

THE ROOM FOR DOUBT

To not build a room for her
is to deny her. The hunger is real.

God-damn it, it's spring,
and I'm dying. I expected abundance.

✦

THE HUNGER

✦

MORNING WORK

Sumac is invasive. It can't be left alone
or out front. Pruners can't control sumac,

and their promise of burning leaves
is best left alone. This is your heart's desire:

Miles makes a tribute to Jack Johnson.
Street music rises up from the garden,

the Mexican father hands his daughter
a pistol and says, *Put it in your purse,*

they'll let us cross with you in the car.
Leaves on fire. Miles makes room

for a guitar and a bass. *Oh, oh,*
the strings repeat, *Oh, no.* Move the sumac

under the Beauty Bush. Put some dahlia's
out front and away from the Japanese Maple.

Let the horn come in when it's ready.
The daughter has her voice, a shiny pistol,

a flaming branch of red leaves.
It isn't even May. Cut it back.

✦

STANDING ALONE, SCREAMING AT THE SKY, GRITO AL CIELO, IN HER OWN VOICE,

M's story:

I can hear the cows coming down
the mountain, ready to struggle
with my uncle. I feel safe here
in the rancho. Why do I feel safe,

knowing the *rancho* is dangerous?

Because once my family started the chain
of killing and revenge, selling the marijuana
on the border to the powerful *gabachos,*

my life has turned to running and hiding.
My father always says, *Mija,*
everything I'm doing I'm doing for you.
My father uses me for drug dealing.

He took me to *Aguililia* so the *Judiciales,*
The FBI, wouldn't search the truck.
My father is armed. It scares me.
He gave me a little .22 to hide under

my blouse for protection. How fun.
My father says, "*Mija* is carrying a gun,
she's *una valientota...*" but how brave was I?
I can't forgive him. I can't trust him.

Sometimes I just want to scream to the sky,
I'm free, that no memory, no revenge
is chasing me, that I'm not the next victim
of my family to get killed. One day I will scream

at the world that I'm free, and not afraid.

✦

Flavors in this salsa remain what they are.
The cucumber doesn't give in to the garlic.
Ginger stands up to the pineapple. The red onion
holds its own, even while sweetened in juices.
The tomato is a tomato. The salsa goes over fish.
The ambition of passion is the drama of the garden.
The idea of courage is not going back.
Our hunger is sufficient fuel.

✦

THE HUNGER

✦

HUNGER IN THE GARDEN

•

TALKING TO MY RAZA

Y's story:

Todos extraños.

Initiation is hard.

I'm learning twice.
I'm getting double from everything.
I'm learning *lo de los gabachos*
and I'm learning *lo de los Mexicanos*
and that's a huge advantage.

•

THERE IS JUST SO MUCH

E's story:

At 6 am I arrive from Seattle.
A 3-hour drive to go to high school.
I had gone to visit my daughter,
check on the house, talk to the lawyers—

this divorce isn't easy. It hurts
to know you committed your life
to someone who changed so dramatically,
to one who shows no mercy. It hurts

not being here. I miss so much.
I am capable of doing everything required.
God has decided to teach me about character.
I'm coming up again, that's important.

Puse las cartas sobre la mesa.
All I need now is for you people
on the other side to give me the chance.

This is where I belong. One day

I'll be back to help others.
Living in two worlds is hard.
Is it an advantage? He is going down.
Los golpes de la vida. Life or death.

My family is all in Mexico.
I miss my mother's *regaños.*
I'm alone with my daughter.
That shakes me. Drastic decisions

drive me crazy. What's best?
Mi fe mueve montañas y eso
es lo que me hace seguir.
Dame los libros sin fronteras.

✦

LA RIQUEZA DE MI GENTE

J's story:

el hombre

Puro remordimiento de conciencia.
Acaba de matar y ya no se aguanta la carga
en su espalda. Pobre hombre.
he was rich in everything—culture,

history, but not anymore. His coraje
made him do it. He has killed.
La calaca is following him,
it is his turn now, this story of este pobre

hombre es riquísima en muchas cosas,
nos dice que el matar te mata,
that we have to appreciate la vida
por ser lo mejor que tenemos hasta ahora.

So many *matanzas, gente que mata por dinero,*
people *que no más por que les da*

su chingada gana. In my town,
in its surroundings, rich and poor,

cut into pieces like vegetables, with *machetes,*
the pieces of meat and bones are put into a *costal,*
and as a final step, thrown into the *canalones*
or the *ríos.* That's how they disappear

without any physical evidence.
Their relatives cry with burning hearts.
El hombre in the story had the chango inside,
but he also had a conscience. *¿Qué changos*

es eso? This may seem negative for *la Raza,*
but it's part of us, *remordimiento*
eating the soul, *venganza* pushed
by the *chaneque, culpa,* accepting the weight

of the consequences. The story makes us rich
not in gold or diamonds, but in feelings.
He shouldn't of killed no one.
The past of my gente is in *mi sangre.*

paso del norte

Crossing *para el otro lado, el norte,*
where we're supposed to find a better life
than in our own *patria. Cruzar* the river,
or *cruzar corriendo. Cruzar* the river.

Some are brought against their will,
but they have to come, they're too young
to defend their thoughts. First we came
to pick *manzanas,* and to work in the fields,

but now more of us come to get an education.
I don't have papers. The power is in the dreams.
The story is rich in truth,
it shows we are capable. My own father

could be the man in the story.
There's also *la pinche migra,*

but we love making fun of it, risking everything.
Nos gusta burlarnos de la migra. La migra

caught me the first time I tried to come here,
but it was an adventure for a 13-year-old boy.
I will never forget *Tijuana* and the running
we had to do to get to *San Isidro. Es que*

somos muy pobres, la riqueza de mi gente.
Sometimes truth is revealed in money.
We will kill for money. You cannot die
of hunger with money.

•

"WHAT'S YOUR STORY, BODEEN?"

I wait for the dream.
I'm in a portable shower
holding a portable phone
waiting for a call from a man

about a book. I wait.
That's my story. I'm naked.
I begin to wake about four,
thinking of you. I try to hold

you and the dream at the same time.
My friend fills his hands with his tears.
I sit with him drinking coffee
while churlish white kids skateboard

across our path. River crossings.
My story is your story. Nothing without you.
My puppy runs down the frisbee
and stops on her way back, drops it,

and shits right in the frisbee.
Fills it up. She's found rotten apples
in the compost while nosing around.
Howl and weep. Waking this morning,

waiting for the phone call, I cross back
to my friend. Maybe Dante is all there is.
Charlie Haden plays a bass so slow
that I get lost in the spaces between

the strings. The melody I discover is mine,
but it isn't, really. I'm a drifter.
Once the boy starts asking questions
he has to take it all the way to God,

and then, past God, to what? Himself.
I listen for you. I can't claim a thing.
I pull weeds in the garden.
I water flowers, listen to music.

•

HERE COME THE IRIS

•

QUEEN OF NO

The beauty of white space.
And the power in No.

In being able to say it,
as a response. No. The charm

in what isn't, what will never be.
What is denied. Hasn't she

been quiet all along?
Distant beloved,

your refusal to speak
makes the poem possible.

Queen of disinterest,
Goddess of Nothing to Say.

Lady of the Eternal Watch,

guachando.

Doesn't the No
give birth to Yes?

Or are they twins?
Born from the same hunger.

✦

LETTER TO LOUISE GLÜCK

✦

Out west all letters are cousins of a lost aunt,
lines as long as empty arroyos, all children
of an ancestor we love so dearly, we clean up
our lives in his absence. I'm in the garden,
but I'm not in myself. So many flowers,
so little of me. All gardens are pretenders.
So much beauty. So many surprises.
Along the path of butterflies and hummingbirds,
I plant a red cabbage and an eggplant
between Mr. Lincoln and the Queen of Iris.
My twin daughters, creations of love,
extremes of yes and no, both with the lessons
of the other before them, appear
with the quietness of the neighborhood cat,
the spring wind creating a storm of blossoms
in the neighbor's cherry tree.
Chance and response. I walk the garden
one more time with a watering can.

✦

Dear Louise,

I'll try to keep this short.
Leave plenty of space.

Ecstatic detachment.
Watch or dream,

my hunger wants all.
Scourging divestment

is a way of going on.
No more. My mother,

in her poverty,
returns more joy

to the world,
than all my pedigreed

flowers planted
in my great ambition.

•

In the Temple of Doubt
do not be misled by Code.

Square corners, plumb lines,
the look of perfection

is a sure sign,
like new paint.

What song is this?
Changing harmonies

wake the dead
and newborn alike.

This garden. These flowers
Not planted for Certitude,

Bitch Goddess
from a seed warehouse,

she doesn't bloom.
But Doubt—

running through nature
and this garden, wild,

unpredictable in great beauty,
surpassing all blueprints

for control, a wilderness.

•

LINES BETWEEN COFFEE AND MUSIC

A birthday poem for Marty Lovins

You were great yesterday in the Temple of Art
pulling Sartre from the cupboard,
Give me a number and I'll answer
any questions on being and nothingness.
Your response to any abstract terror is to laugh.
Doubt doesn't think anything's funny.
Happy Birthday. Today you're 58?
Doubt is juice I can count on.
You love the beauty in any surprise,
contrary juices in the unpredictable.
Yesterday I catch myself worrying over outcomes,
not the trite shit administrators trade for,
but the bigger worry, *Will my loved ones be safe?*
Efrén tells me his family will bring his Aunt and niece
across the border. *Will they be safe?* I ask.
No problem, Efrén says. The *Coyote costs $1700 for my aunt,*
and we'll bring her little girl across as my sister.
I love the trail Efrén cuts into the narrow line of the border.
The wilderness inside. It's all borderlands now.
You're Dada in these parts, Lovins.
The condom rots in your assemblage on the gallery walls.
Among all that beauty, surrounded by all that polished gold,
you ask those walking through art to open their eyes.
Being careful is what you are with a file.
Being careful won't keep anything from rotting.

May 15, 1997

BOOK SIX

The Summer Garden

...that if one loved one's own landscape it would then, and only then, be possible to love other landscapes.
Robert Adams

Book Six

BARKING AT THE SAXOPHONE

Lacy hears the music when my truck
turns onto Bell from 14th. By the time
I get to the Poetry Pole, she's barking
for Coltrane, a dog whose only purpose

is to receive what I send out. Useless.
Pleasureful dog. Dream retriever.
Lacy takes the frisbee from the sky
at top speed over her right shoulder,

a sprinter. Black dog. River of joy,
turning everything I carry into grace
with a turn of her head, taking the disc,
the spinning, loaded disc, sailing from

my arms, back into her certain,
carefully bred mouth. Lacy, silk thread,
seamless explosion of energy. Effortless
performance. Coltrane moistens the reed,

embarking, leaving behind the rest;
Lacy, reunited with desire, claiming the frisbee,
circles the park in triumph.
Lacy can hear Coltrane coming.

Dreamwalker and Coltrane.
Athletes in love. Far from us. Far.
A truck turns a corner onto a street
trafficking only in music.

•

Mid afternoon on Memorial Day.
Karen cuts peonies from the garden.
Mom calls from Seattle. Her favorite
third basemen of all-time, Jimmy Presley,
was back in the Kingdome, in uniform
for old-timer's day. *Remember, Jimmy,*
we were there, August 16, 1981 when
he hit the home run in the bottom of the 9th
to beat the Yankees. The failure
of Christianity is here, in the authenticity
of the moment, old people
experience themselves more completely
at baseball games. I set my coffee down
by M's senior photo. *My father murders people.*
It's not easy to say. I make my pack lighter
in this room. It's a rest stop.
The garden matures. I miss the violence
of making rich beds, hauling rock.
The Beauty Bush in blossom.
Barry pins Ginsberg's Vomit of the Tiger
to the Poetry Pole. I catch him with the camera.
Snapshot. White t-shirt, red Phillies cap.
Surrounded by flowers. Sacramental companions.
Ginsberg always carried a camera.
We knew these moments were disappearing.
We experienced each other as eternal.
Most of my students are illegal.
Does this surprise you? Karen asks.
These lines witness to something, but what?
Laying on the grass looking up at the stars,
I say to Karen, *I can't imagine a higher calling.*
I have never had such students, or so many.
No, I wasn't prepared for the beauty or the surprise.

•

Members of the Iris Society want me to mark
the rhizomes with a marking pen, but I can't do it.
My history went another direction
when I let new canes in the old roses

take over the marking system
and naming was left to memory alone.
These ladies have taught me to divide and plant,
to soak the rhizome in bleach, to discard the old
to promote new blooms. Hiking and biking
along country roads, even in city streets,
they have a lookout for clumps of antiques
in someone's backyard, or in weeds on vacant lots.
Hardy, dependable, beautiful. Survivors,
the woman says, *under rugged conditions.*
Nameless heirlooms,
passed through families.
This is what we stand for, she says.

Women know.
Oh, God, Janeen says,
walking through the path of butterflies,
Look at those pinks.
The iris are here.
They don't last, Lena says.
I want them here all summer.
Monet cables Clemenceau in Paris
Get over to Giverny now. The iris are here.
Shut it down! Shut down the government!
These days.

◆

It depends on what you know.

◆

FOLLOWING LACY

The dog took me inside. I followed her.
I can't talk about it in time.
Time makes no sense.
I follow her, now, outside.

She takes me to the park.
We go to the river.

I throw her the bumper,
or the ball. Frisbee

is why she's here.
She's called to the frisbee.
I carry the camera,
try to catch her in mid-air.

✦

WILD FACE

My friend comes by the house and pins a tribute
to Ginsberg on the Poetry Pole. I take a photo of him
with the camera. I write it into the poem.
Barry wears a white t-shirt and a red Phillies hat.
This is the photo I describe in the poem.
In the picture there is no hat.
I like that, he says. I like that.

There's a woman in my head and it's not me.
It's the damnedest thing.
And the cat.
The cat's meowing at night on the off hour.
It's like a dentist's drill.
This morning catches me like a push from behind.
My wife says she's going to steer clear of me today.

In this story, the boy clears the room by cutting a fart
like the Colorado River creating the Grand Canyon in one blast.
I ask a young Mexican about the word in Spanish.
He uses it in a sentence, *No la hagas de pedo—*
Don't make a big deal out of it—it's only hot air.
Santana always turns towards the lipstick.
Revenge wasn't meant for those caught in the crossfire.

Getting my eyes dilated, I ask the doctor,
How were you called to the eye?
I liked small things, he says.
Big things that can't be seen.
All the flowers in the garden are distorted.
Yes, I wanted bacteriology when med school opened up

and I didn't have to go to Korea.

All the stools are standing on their heads.
I snap a photo of Lovins counting days,
listening to tunes coming from the cupboard.
The world is already Golden Ash.
I don't really know what's in the photos,
but the guys in my pictures, the ones with wild face,
they could tell you things.

May 30, 1997

✦

AT THE HISPANIC ACHIEVER'S AWARD BANQUET

Every obstacle in the way
is part of the curriculum.
We all want to be here and everybody wants us.
Everyone is legal and on scholarship.

We praise our lives
because we've all come this far.
David Gutiérrez, Miriam López, Eva Siddhartha Valdivia.
Jacqueline Hernández.
Four standing.

We're here.

Even praise can't say it, alabanza, or sing it.

Everyone is thankful.
We take these odds.
We are one *pueblo,*
barrio unido.
There is no division.
The mayor is a homeboy.
Alcalde como vato loco.
Every scholarship is big. *Becas grandes para todos.*
Everyone has papers.

We dress up in our hope.

We don't answer any questions.
No shadows, only the flashing,
and the lights of our cameras.

The patrón is who he is.
We go to school.
Our Social Security cards are our own.
We're surrounded by truth.

✦

LINES ON THE RETIREMENT OF A CENTRAL ADMINISTRATOR

–For Frank Naasz

Check my new claim, the Vato says,
making a circle with his thumb and index finger
on his right hand, then crossing it
with two fingers of his left. I look at him for more.
Break the chain, he says. Rompe las cadenas,
that's one of our refrains in Latino Lit,
but what makes the freedom possible is the books.
I was in the principal's office when I overheard
the Curriculum Director say she signed off
on those books you bought us, claiming those
for the curriculum that doesn't exist.
Working with *la Raza.* I want to tell you
in your last month, after a long career,
what these books mean. Listen to the essays
kids wrote this week, then read to each other yesterday:

We live in two extremes. The Mexican and the American.
It's hard to find the real person.
To know who you are you need to know who lives in you.
That's Yoshimi. Her sister Alma writes
about the Iguana Killer. *I like this story best*
because iguanas, unlike humans, can see in every direction.
They're writing on the stories of Alberto Rios,
the new book we fought for last fall.
The book you bought.
Alma's telling us: Open your eyes.
I know I'm a new beginning.

I can check everything.

Frank, this is the geography of the imagination.
We're carving out a country we can carry with us.
In this third country todos son bienvenidos,
todos somos todos. We can see each other rising
from different grounds, in Alma's words,
we no longer have to think of belonging only to one.
Alma speaks for us. She wants Heaven.

I am the bracera. I am the India. I am the wife.
I am the woman I'm inventing.
I am a totally different river.

Gabino Salazar writes: Let me underline all these words.
It tells us something true in the life. Gabino
is full-blooded Mixtec, Oaxaqueño. He translates
his day for his mother from English and Spanish,
into Mixtec. Gabino writes, *I think this story*
is the most beautiful story I've heard in my life.
This character is never embarrassed about his home.

Frank, you bought these books.

Let me close with some words from Samuel Barrera:
Wherever we go we belong, because we are citizens
of the world, and we belong, not only in Mexico, or USA,
but in all countries of this planet, because I'm 'hermano'
of who wants me to be just friend, of who believes in me,
shows me how to behave, I have thousands of 'hermanos.'

Frank, carry these words from Yoshimi into your new life:

I make a way where there is no way.
I've thrown away what I don't need in my bag.
I'm not afraid anymore.

When you were principal at Martin Luther King Elementary,
you wanted a popcorn machine for your kids.
You went out and bought it.

Abrazos, hermano, *abrazos.*

THE EXHAUSTION

and the things I didn't catch
cut me off at the knees. *You better*

git hit in your soul stories.
Oh, Mingus. Charlie Mingus—

At a soccer game, Garcilazo,
mi compañero,

takes *a golpe*
to the head and goes down

not knowing he's scored.
Each outburst of sound,

an exploding metaphor.
The end of a year

calls up all of the celebrated
grief. Gabino gives me his mother's

name and pueblo in Oaxaca.
Nieves Lopes Reyes. Rio Verde,

San Juan Mixtepec, Tlixiaco.
Alma's been writing graffiti

on the walls of my heart all year.
I take a snapshot of Lovins

to put on my wall. Taking the roll
of film to the developer, I see

another roll on the window sill,
and put it in my pocket.

Pods from the poppies growing
in my garden make a tea promising

only pleasure. I can grind them

in the coffee grinder. Knowing this

is enough to make me a felon.
The dark heart of the blossom

blossoms. It always depends
on what you know. Last night

I worked into the night
working on a woman's book

that took me out of myself,
the promise in the tea. Writing

has no value in transmitting
magic. The gods of life

die only to rise again.
Those who resist are punished.

Savage animals never kill
for pleasure. The god teaches

man to disregard man's laws
in order to rediscover divinity.

The summer garden gives
the gardener a rest. Oh, *Karen,*

to spend another summer
dreaming with you! Now

is the hour of Delphinium,
and the great vertical petals

filtering the light creating
a new transparency.

Love will do nothing
with organization. Oh,

to be a pilgrim seeking

the mystical bird. The wall

of memory covers
and recovers while I take

my coffee. Magic berry.
Abstinence alters the mind.

And film itself changing signs.
The puppy always knows

what she wants. Javier writes,
to eat *nachos, a comer* almonds,

I only had to jump on the tree
behind our *gallinero.* My uncle

was married to one of the many
sisters of my *jefecita's* mother.

Last night I swallowed the stars.
He has earned the images

in his abandonment of self.
Now, he too, knows who he is,

now he knows what he has been
called to do. *Do not betray*

your calling abrecamino,
hermano, carnal, m'ijo.

The film in the flower.
The film in the camera.

In this house, on this morning,
Soma runs through the music.

Parables, dreams, visions.
La pinche migra is only

a traffic cop to the gods.

The film sitting on my

window sill for two years
is full of Lovins, and his work

hammering jewels
for the hearts of poets.

The film has been rolling
for two years waiting for me.

I have placed his work
on the poems themselves.

I throw the frisbee
as far as I can throw it

and the pup brings it back.
Dream retrieval, images

lost and found. The camera
around my neck releases me.

•

The bass player wonders
what's going to happen next,
but he doesn't let go of the string.
He's holding back to make the song.

The bass player knows how to listen.
The best lover is the one who listens.
The deepest penetration is in the song.

•

BALL IN THE BOWL

The black dog barks for the ball.
It's too hot to run, but she can't help herself.
She wants to go. She turns into her kennel
for a drink of water and drops the ball

in the bowl. She wants two things at once.
She always does. Even now she wants the frisbee
in the park. This game of catch is for me.
It's what she does for me
between work and the park.
She plays catch while I drink my Coke
in the garden, while I sit on the bench
in a daze, destroyed again by all these stories.

◆

1997

A perfect mirror.
A day with no shadows.
Living the 20th Century
a day at a time.

1997

◆

The first number is a day.
The second number is a year.
I water whatever wants water.
What these beds want
is a man to go through them
with a hoe. Lacy breaks
towards me in joy
with the frisbee in her mouth,
and a woman watching us
calls over to me,
I'd come to that voice myself.
Flowers need pruning.
Karen identifies 1000 grape plants
coming up in the iris bed.
Seeds from the jelly
of memory and forgetting
that didn't destroy themselves
in my compost. Dionysus
teaches the dance and music
that leads to ecstasy.

Karen takes me
and asks me if I've voted
for the Stadium, says
she going to punch a hole
in my ballot. Shiva said,
I am not distinct from the phallus.
Meditating on this pleasure
we free ourselves from future lives.

•

I make Karen a latte, ask her
if she can see the Dreamwalker
from where she sits. She nods.
All night dreaming, waking stoned
from the rich Soma pouring into my cup.
On this morning we praise what is.
This is prayer. The horn
in the garden is Wynton's.
A way is always open for man
to return to the divine plan.
Soma is God's sperm. Seed thoughts.
A puppy walks in roses.

•

There is nothing to keep me from the poem
this morning but me. If I call up
what is in me, it will be found.
I must value my work in order to offer it.
The Poetry Pole in the garden is a pathway for energy.
Two poems by Judy, a purple Bachelor Button,
and a photo of Barry pinning a poem to the Pole
have been offered up. Yesterday was a day
set aside for fathers. I am not elsewhere.
Stretching, my children pulled me into their world.
Karen sits at the top of the stairs
and pulls on her nylons. She sees me
sitting here and says, I thought you left.

•

Looking down the path of butterflies and hummingbirds
from the back yard with a handful of cherries,
the puppy in my head, her black river of a body
recovering from her work with the frisbee,—
such reaching for heaven.
A white car pulls up fast on Bell. A woman gets out
of her car, and goes straight for the Poetry Pole.
Like she knows what she's wants. Judy's two poems,
The Mole, and Want, pinned and alone for a week,
with a couple of purple Bachelor Buttons. The woman
does not see me looking at her reading. It is not uncommon
to find readers at the Pole. Yet I have been surprised
by her, dressed in her rich suit and expensive hair,
and it takes me some time to remember
these poems are for her, and I call the pup
into the house. I watch her from the kitchen,
standing before the Pole, leaning into the poems,
and I know, violating her own prayers,
this is about desire, Judy's two poems making
direct contact. This moment is pivotal
in all of our lives. I know what's in these poems
is in all poems, and I know, now, this Pole,
placed in an outpost off any known path,
promises what we're all looking for, and this woman
pulling up fast and easy before it, finds it.

✦

Sitting on the bench in the Garden Room
I point the camera through the delphinium
and the tree roses to the Poetry Pole.
The late afternoon sun shines off the cedar,
the cut letters P O E T R Y, raised to the lens
by the shadows within. The light changes.
In the mornings the letters to the east
catch a different sun. Bachelor Buttons
coming up from seed threaten to take the Pole
out of the sun. The camera in this morning
light catches something new in each shot.
The light gets behind the paper.
The paper takes on the reflection of flowers.
The paper is a sail in the wind.

In spring rain the poem bleeds.
It turns to parchment under the drying sun.
One can map the changes of a single poem.
One can keep track of the odd visitor.
The camera knows nothing of which direction
the energy flows, or its pull on me.
I change the poems on the Pole.
I place the exposed and weathered poems
in a room by themselves. They take on
the texture of parchment.
The pile of photos in the living room grows.

•

THE POETRY POLE IN THE GARDEN

Fence poles surrounding Neruda's house
at Isla Negra become a memorial
in their poverty, in offering themselves
to weather, as an outpost far from the seats
of power, in the manner in which they have withstood
the terrorism of Pinochet and Nixon.
They have become notebooks for those
who would travel so far to see grand waves
knocking against rocks found in famous poems,
and collected surreal images of the well-traveled poet,
for in looking up, before entering the grounds,
one notices the letters, left like flowers,
pressed into windswept wooden poles,
sentries. Witnesses. Often, in our grieving,
thinking we must act, that we're procrastinating,
we don't see our grief work as making a way.
I weep before the fence poles at Isla Negra,
puzzled and affirmed by the effortless Fuck You
to power brokers, the soft manner
in which the seeming dull pencil penetrates wood,
leaving lasting impressions.

The raising of a pole is a meritorious act.
It should be raised preferably in isolated places or on mountains.
Ancient sanctuaries are usually found outside cities.
Shiva's symbol is the linga, or phallus.

The linga is everywhere in the garden.
Sperm carries the ancestral heritage.
Man is only a phallus-bearer, servant of his sexual organ.
The Pole is an outward sign. A symbol.
It is like this garden some see driving by
on their way to the Medical Center.
There is another garden, too. The garden inside.
There are two poles. The subtle pole is internal.
The purpose of the phallic image
is to stir the faithful towards knowing.
Those who are not yet conscious worship the physical.

•

The garden is a privileged place,
out of time, like birth places
connecting visible to invisible.
I can feel Harry Rinarder, here, this morning,
remembering how he walked me through his azaleas
before paying me for cutting his lawn.
Mine is a summer garden of jazz.
Jackie McClean plays here. He talks to me.
When I heard Ornette,
that was the first saxophone player
I'd heard who stepped into that room,
the big room of freedom.
The laurel, the vine and the ivy
are the sacred plants of Dionysus.
The grapes against the Press threaten to bring
down the gutters with their tenacious climbing.
Nearly all remedies and poisons come from plants.
Pods from four poppies ground up in the coffee grinder
and made into a simple tea
contain enough opium for two weeks of dreams.
Poisons, drugs, and passions combine to tackle the gods.
Plants know immediately what's going on
with the man walking through the garden.
The plant always responds.

•

In the listening room it's all music.

•

MAKING MEANING

When I laugh at the woman
I am only laughing at what she said.
She can only see the text in front of her.
Raúl writes me a poem with this line,
tengo el libro invisible conmigo,
yo siempre estoy leyendo.
Give me this invisible book.
Asking for a copy of his poem
for the Poetry Pole, I know how
uncertain this all seems to the frightened.
Keith Jarrett plays the Koln Concert
in the Garden Room, every blossom applauds.
Drinking one cup of poppy tea
defines my summer.
This dark heart from the poppy
growing across the path from the Pole.
Did I trespass in the garden of the gods?
After the music this morning
I must live in the world of men.
Today is solstice. No shadows.
Barry brings me a book for my birthday
six weeks away, Reading Jazz.
Bonnie writes from Boston.
She has been with Kuranamayi,
the Goddess of Music and Knowledge.
Amma, as she is affectionately called.
She gave her blessing to the people
and to our house as she drove by.
That night Bonnie dreams.
She sees me in a new place.
I write to Bonnie from this new room.
Karen calls for flowers.
We are always making meaning, all of us,
even this woman who I do not understand.
Perhaps my laughter will help her to see.

PUTTING RAÚL'S POEM ON THE POLE

—Soy el sueño de mi madre
También fui su pesadilla.
—Raúl Torres

Exacto, Camarada. Exacto.
It's not that grapefruit I took from my lunch sack
and held before you, you naming it,
Río Red, taking it from my hands, telling me
which field in Texas it came from,
el valle Río Grande, hermano del Yakima,
not that, that binds us to the same story.
No es el sabor que yo tengo
para la pinche palabra verde.
Tampoco no es porque
tú escribes poemas con el
seudónimo "Torito."

Good words for me make connections.
Hermano, compadre, carnal, compañero.
Words scorned by the *patrones*
even as they come from their mouths.
In the poem you gave me last week,
you give me one more, *camarada,*
closing a circle of protection, knowing
these words of affection have been terrorized
by Zapatistas machine-gunning peasants in Chiapas,
the last word they'll ever hear. Words we exchange
in poems, the forum for knowing.
Words the pendejos y pendejas
en los trajes y corbatas entienden
and know how to use, *Hermano*
being the favorite of the Christian Fundamentalist.
¿Cómo llegamos a la linea entre los lados?
Your truth beginning this poem is mine, too.
The dream, and the nightmare.
Living in two worlds takes us invisibly.
Meaning comes in the tantras,
the sounds and gestures made

at the invisible points, connecting us
to multiple others we don't understand.
The dream and the nightmare.
Abrazos, tu compa, tu camarada.

BOOK SEVEN

In The Listening Room

Such fragile moss in a massive tree
Portland City Bus

Book Seven

IN THE LISTENING ROOM,

it's all music. Listening is all there is.
Karen turns off the sink upstairs.
Lifting the arm of the phonograph
my daughter says, Nobody listens
to records anymore. Putting the needle down
on the red vinyl, brings back Tony Fruscella,
playing His Master's Voice, give him more room.
This is understated stuff, intimate, a bit sad—
the essence of cool, New York style, 1955.
Making a tape in the living room,
my daughter says, Nobody listens to tapes.
Carrying the music into the garden
I listen.
The Poetry Pole rejecting nothing.

✦

CHINA AND DENMARK

—Lines for Bonnie

A way to begin a letter.
As a gift to Denmark.

Sitting in the Garden Room
looking through three tree Roses,

Mr. Lincoln, to the Poetry Pole,
I see a China Rose beyond in blossom.

Kierkegaard, neglected in Denmark,
leaves the pews empty. I will have

nothing to do with dogma
having turned my life over to the dream.

Bonnie writes, *China and Denmark.*
She dreams. I find the beginning

of her letter only when I look for more.
Cold Mountain cuts a poem into stone.

•

I follow the Path of the Mailman
and count on it for the music arriving daily.
News of your dream greets me
sitting surrounded by flowers and jazz.
You and Pete have been called.
You are dreaming.
You are traveling to China.
You will take your violin.
It is a rising kite.
Black-eyed Susans coming up from seed
by the Clematis become the protector of the fragile vine.
Plants responding immediately to water
listen to music mingling
with our chants into the night.
The Crescent Moon, the cup of Soma,
worn on the forehead of Shiva,
pours itself into our parched ears.
The elixir of life, feared by many,
pours into our ears as tonic, not poison.
Blake stands in front of the door to Jerusalem.
Holding the sun in his hand as a lamp
about to enter the shadowy city.
There is always a woman
in Denmark or Boston
who will never believe in China.
Another woman in Yakima wants it on a map.
The businessman and the preacher
carry cigarettes and Bibles.

No one told Cold Mountain to write poems,
but you were told to make music.
The woman in Denmark understands all this.
What she won't tolerate is the imagination.

⁎

Coltrane plays from the impulse years.
The left hand of God has always been for writing poems.
There's no quit in the old dog tonight.
The pup's tongue is bloody from catching the frisbee.
The moral law is only social convention.
Charlie Haden lets the others take the lead.
Her dry tongue uttered inspired words.
He's the bass player in the back.
It's necessary to know how to change directions.
He's making all this music music.
One must become what one is devoted to, musician.
The way of the left hand is beyond good and evil.

⁎

Some mornings I forget about him.
He just stands and plays.
Him and that saxophone.
I'll be in and out, back from the store.
He's playing all the time.
His cup is never empty.
His music just keeps coming.

⁎

KEEPER OF THE HOUSE

House keeper. *Portero.*
The simple inversion of words.

This morning I'm on my knees,
waxing floors, something

I did as a child with my mother
in North Dakota. Mom let me

skate in my socks for helping.
Out west Mom cleaned houses

for others, while I kept ours.
If things were clean...

Mom didn't have a machine
for polishing. She never

thought of this deep cleaning
as prayer, celebration.

•

Get up in the cab, Lacy,
I say, just as she steps in dog shit
left by the neighbor's dog.

Some mornings
start with dog shit
tracked all over your truck.

•

Karen tells me the neighbor lady
came into the bank. There are bills
after the husband's heart attack.
We sit in the car talking after a movie.
They've never had a bill, always paid cash.
Insurance pays 80 per cent,
but there's nothing left for the house payment.
Data bases on the Net
let people know they're in trouble.
Realtors want to help them sell the house.
I showed her how to refinance.
It's good she could trust you to talk.

•

I take the pork chops and a plate
of tropical fruit leftover from Karen's party.
A man says we pay for any meat, we don't kill ourselves.

Any point of view that leaves out our cruelty
sees a mirage. This morning promises
only long solos of Coltrane. I do get it.
The sheets of sounds, the music arriving
on multiple levels, the man standing and breathing,
playing for what comes up, settling
into one river of ascending or descending sound.
I pour juice from the pineapple and mango
onto the pork chops, squeeze lime,
and add garlic. The music's coming all the time.
I have been released from good and evil.
From seeking justice.
There's more passion now.
I feel where Coltrane's trying to go.
I'll cook those pork chops slow, in wood smoke.

The smoke drifts through the garden
mixing with the saxophone.
I am pruning in the roses.
The long stems from the spent blossoms
offer their throats. Flowers know.
The knife's blade is clean.
I get back in the way that I take.
I am being watched while I cut.

•

Half-wind, half brass,
this shaman, warm and powerful
al mismo tiempo, straddles two worlds,

waiting for Coleman Hawkins.
No novelty now. Sprung, fully armed.
His Body & Soul, from 3000,

most popular American song.
The saxophone waits for the men
in the middle who know

both sides, who will carve
an entire world from this border—
lines of sound, bridges

between what we know,
and what knows us, the dream
erasing boundaries.

⬩

The jazz writers—
outlaws, *correvedeles.*
Go-betweens can't tell you why,
enchanted only with what it is,
what they've seen and heard at night—
paid to bring back a story they love
more than their wives, more than papers
they write for, more than bylines,
like the jazzmen they listen to,
more than themselves.

⬩

THE HOUSE IN THE HEART

—for Carolyn after putting her poem on the Poetry Pole

Believing it's music
is the work

one does listening.
When I listen,

I am only devotion.
Devotion makes the way.

Nothing illicit.
Nothing is absurd

when I listen.
When I listen

it's all music,
me and the world.

•

A song, a saxophone and a voice.
All three working on each other

build this house. Of course
it's empty. The emptiness

makes it all possible:
the garden, the house,

the listening room.
Now you can hear music.

•

In 1957 John Coltrane had this dream,
he was in it, but he was watching it at the same time.
The whole band is playing in this room.
A room made for him.
He doesn't know if he is playing,
but I felt the band was mine.
It is just a matter of getting to the bandstand.
He can't see the future but he knows.
He says, *I knew this was coming.*
He says it another way, *I felt this was coming.*

•

Don't be afraid.
What you call emptiness
is only a room for music.

This joy is for you.
Remember what it feels like
so you can return.

Don't be alarmed.
What you hear
is only yourself.
No room here
for striving.

Achievers are bored.

In this place
a voice is born.
Carolyn, Carolyn.

•

JULY 2, 1997

Karen looks in my eye
and thinks she sees a pimple.
I think it's probably dog shit.
I cut her a bowl of cantaloupe
and watermelon for breakfast.
Driving through
the Columbia River Gorge
on Sunday with Karen
and the pup, we stop
to let Lacy go after the ball,
to swim in the current
of the largest river.
At the new museum I watch
an 8 millimeter movie
of the Yakamas fishing
over the falls at Celillo
before the dam was built.
Fishermen walk on the wet planks,
water crashing on all sides,
with loose ropes around their waists.
In the dark light of the museum
I get dizzy. Counting the days,
counting calendar, iti tá mat,
I think of the string records
of Sally Jackson. Over 1,577 knots,
35 feet of leather and hemp,
where she placed 226 markers
in red, blue and pink yarn,
nights and days,
beginning her life
after the death of her husband.
So much is underwater.

So much blossoms on this garden.
I sit with Cy looking into the lilies.
He is telling me what Jesus said.
He says, *My Dad used to say,*
Come here, Cy, let me wipe
that cat shit out of your eyes.
Karen is so lovely in her summer dress
and her dark sun glasses
leaving for work, waving goodby,
saying she won't be home for lunch.

•

But every movement
generates a vibration
and therefore a sound
that is peculiar to it.
A sound
may not be audible
to our ears,
but it exists as pure sound.

Yesterday the thick ears were mine.
I couldn't hear.

A litter of stray kittens
making a home under the patio
play with a sheet of plastic,
the sounds coming to me
from beneath my feet
in the kitchen. The universe
is that which moves.

A scratching vibration.

I walk Mesatchee Creek Trail
with the Dreamwalker to the American River
where it is too high to ford. Too green to see.
Cut loose from any leash but my song in her name,
Lacy Dreamwalker, the athlete in river form
winds towards me through fallen timber
stretching out over fallen logs

her belly open to upturned punji sticks from the broken branches,
clearing the blades by the margin
of our combined breaths.

I hear where this is going.

Back to the first vowel.
Back to the first consonant.

The barely perceptable comma

slicing light between the belly and the knife.

Afterward

On his journey from North Dakota to Seattle to Viet Nam to Chile and ultimately to Yakima, Jim Bodeen has accomplished something remarkable: he has learned who he is and grown comfortable with that understanding. "I experience the self as nothing. I am not inferior. Response to what has been given is all." This is the way he puts it in sHADOWmARKED lines on a broadside of the poem titled "In the Mari Sandoz Crazy Horse Camp..." that also opens his recent book, *Impulse to Love.*

This House is about, among many other things, "the geography of the imagination." In Eastern Washington, especially Yakima County where this poetry was written, and Walla Walla County where it is published, the geography of the imagination is coming more and more to include the beautiful and revivifying tones and sounds of Spanish.

Mixing his dreams, his work, his family, his Labrador Lacy Dreamwalker, his students, his love of music, his friends and his literary antecedents into immensely compassionate poetry, is an act of faith in his stated belief that "all poems are spiritual." He writes what is possible with what he is given. In the course of a cycle he was taken up in a spell with the first stanza and released with the last line, ten months later. Only the whole of life finally matters and in Bodeen's hands the common objects of our existence are suffused with warm intelligence.

The poetry goes in many directions at dream speed. Sometimes he wants to "Retain the conversational tone to project / the irrational image." Other times he turns into a receptacle and "When the dream speaks, I listen." Often as not he lets his friends and students speak for themselves as "The only fear I have / is the fear my mother gives me," or "The idea of courage is not going back. / Our hunger is sufficient fuel." The overall effect is to recreate the carefully woven fabric of our life.

A publisher as well as a poet of renown, he has time even for the ironic terror of the poetry business noting, "This is literature / that means business;" or "Not a single book will enter Barnes & Noble without a Bar Code;" or implicating his wife Karen into the mix, "Going to make her stand up for poetry / in a roomful of suits."

Way beyond the business of poetry is the actual business of poetry. Teaching at Davis High School in Yakima, someday to be renamed Ray Carver High—the library already has a Ray Carver Center—Bodeen knows that "The new culture will come from the ashes of this one." We are in a phrase "Gabachos getting to know who we are."

Eastern Washington is only two congressional districts wide but a major cultural fusion is now taking place here and everywhere else in the putative United States, especially say, Texas, Colorado and California, where the hard-working vitality and élan of the rapidly developing Hispanic contributions are gradually shaming the rest of us into a deeper understanding of both our past and our future. Foremost among these contributions is their love of and reliance on family as the primary institution.

"Nothing on earth / is more contemptible // than borders." Bodeen erases the borders, phrase by musical phrase, with a fine eye for detail and with gracious humility. Notice what happens when he lets his students—"Most of my students are illegal,"—speak for themselves as in "At the Hispanic Achiever's Award Banquet:"

> Every obstacle in the way
> is part of the curriculum.
> We all want to be here and everybody wants us.
> Everyone is legal and on scholarship...
>
> We are one *pueblo,*
> *barrio unido.*
> There is no division.
> The mayor is a homeboy.
> *Alcalde como vato loco.*
> Every scholarship is big. *Becas grandes para todos.*
> Everyone has papers...

Our Social Security cards are our own.
We're surrounded by truth.

How sweet it will be when we all get it straight. The terrible exploitation has to cease. The sickening news out of Yakima this morning is that the INS is planning to "roundup" between 750 and 1,400 "illegal" migrant workers for the purpose of harassing, intimidating and deporting them. Roundup is a cattle prod phrase used by fascists too decadent and disorganized to pick their own fruit. It ought to be enough to make you choke on the apple in your mouth.

Bodeen quotes Gabino Salazar, Mixtec from Oaxaca: "I think this story / is the most beautiful story I've ever heard in my life. / This character is never embarrassed about his home."

So what is this "home" we hear so much about and where might it be located? Bodeen has written a poem into the future. It is a poem about who we are becoming and what we are doing here. What we are doing here is, "We're carving out a country we can carry with us. / In this third country *todos son bienvenidos, / todos somos todo.*" You'll be bigger and warmer for feeling this poem. Bienvenidos a *This House*.

Charles Potts
Walla Walla
February 19, 1999

Author's Note:

I wanted to write a single poem about a single morning. I wanted to be in the garden listening to *In This House, On This Morning* by the Wynton Marsalis Septet. What I found is that I was supposed to write a poem larger than I had intended.

Everything else is in the poem, except to say that Rob Prout and I have worked together for years at Davis High School and it's all been good. This book along with his photography, has brought us closer together. We've taken some pretty good looks into the canyon.

From a conversation with the photographer, Rob Prout:

I'm looking for a match, a recognition, a connection–
between a seed that's been there, and something else.

In the physical world. With the other world. The unconscious one.

Yes, so when I drive by,
I'm looking for connections, And I hope that it finds me.

And there are other times of pure discovery, but I have
a feeling that the seeds are just a deeper connection
of something that's already been there.

There are times that I have to stop and pull over.
If I have my camera, it's really good.